CONSUMER CULTURE IN AMERICA

Consumer Culture in America

Spectacle, Deception, Simulation and Illusion in the Marketplace

Wilber W. Caldwell

Algora Publishing
New York

Library of Congress Cataloging-in-Publication Data

Names: Caldwell, Wilber W., author.
Title: Consumer culture in America : a guide to consumerism / by Wilber W.
　Caldwell.
Description: New York : Algora Publishing, [2024] | Includes
　bibliographical references and index. | Summary: "The swiftly evolving
　American consumer culture has made us willing converts to a new value
　system — the worship of the toys and leisure, wealth, and the perpetual
　expansion of the economic sphere. Our popular culture pulls everything
　into its orbit. We are losing sensitivities in the realms of social
　justice, war, human exploitation, and the fragility of the natural
　world"— Provided by publisher.
Identifiers: LCCN 2024047600 (print) | LCCN 2024047601 (ebook) | ISBN
　9781628945515 (trade paperback) | ISBN 9781628945522 (hardcover) | ISBN
　9781628945539 (pdf)
Subjects: LCSH: Consumption (Economics)—Moral and ethical aspects—United
　States. | Consumer behavior—United States. | Capitalism—Moral and
　ethical aspects—United States. | Popular culture—United States.
Classification: LCC HB835 .C28 2024 (print) | LCC HB835 (ebook) | DDC
　339.470973—dc23/eng/20241007
LC record available at https://lccn.loc.gov/2024047600
LC ebook record available at https://lccn.loc.gov/2024047601

Printed in the United States

TABLE OF CONTENTS

PREFACE   1

CHAPTER ONE: PRISONERS OF CONSUMERISM   3
    The King of Prussia   3
    Prisoners of Consumerism   5
    Analysis by Example   8
    Cracker Barrel   10
    McDonald's   13
    BrandsMart   18

CHAPTER TWO: A BRIEF HISTORY OF CONSUMER CULTURE   23
    A Thankfully Brief Discussion of Marxian Commodity Fetishism   23
    The Origins of Consumer Culture   25
    The Development of Consumer Culture   27
    Some Early Examples of Consumer Culture   30
    Walter Benjamin and Charles Baudelaire   33
    Max Horkheimer and Theodor Adorno   38
    John Kenneth Galbraith and Daniel Bell   41
    Modernism and Postmodernism   42
    Jean-François Lyotard and Jean Baudrillard   44

CHAPTER THREE: REINVENTING OURSELVES IN THE MARKETPLACE   49
   The Quest for Individual Style   49
   Emancipation and Consumer Culture   56
   Depthlessness and Atomization in Consumer Culture   59
   Domination and Consumer Culture   61

CHAPTER FOUR: MEDIA CULTURE   63
   Television: Creating Model Citizens   63
   Television's Brief Journey from the Real to the Unreal   67
   Television, Media Culture, and Consumer Culture   70

CHAPTER FIVE: VIRTUAL REALITY AND CONSUMER CULTURE   77
   Cyberculture, Simulation, and Consumer Culture   77
   Consumer Culture in the Age of Information   80
   Celebrity, Individuality, and the Changing Face of Fame   83
   Celebrities and Consumers: Critical Readings   87
   The Breadth of the Celebrity World   89
   Celebrity and Hyper-reality   96

CHAPTER SEVEN: CONSUMER CULTURE AND EVERYDAY LIFE   99
   The Aesthetic of the Everyday   99
   Beyond Individualism   104

CHAPTER EIGHT: THE IDEOLOGY CONSUMER CULTURE   107
   Defining Ideology   107
   Consumer Culture and the Ideology of American Individualism   110
   Consumer Culture and the Ideology of American Capitalism   114
   The Ideology of Consumer Culture   118
   Leisure, Spending, Luxury, and Consumer Culture   121

CHAPTER NINE: AMERICAN INDIVIDUALISM AND THE PARADOX OF CONSUMER
   CULTURE   127
   A Chronicle of American Individualism   127
   Individualism and Ambiguity in Consumer Culture   128
   The Paradox of Consumer Culture   131

BIBLIOGRAPHY   135

INDEX   141

PREFACE

This book explores modern American consumer culture and seeks to unmask its complex and often hidden workings. As contemporary American popular culture swiftly expands and evolves, an attendant consumer culture has blossomed in the fertile soil of American consumerism. This new culture of the commodity has sparked considerable attention and debate. Accordingly, to avoid some of the confusion produced by ongoing controversies, let's begin by establishing a few broad definitions.

By **popular culture**, I mean that eclectic collection of widespread practices, cultural products, beliefs, and objects distinguished by their broad presence across economic, ethnic, social, and regional groups.

By **consumer culture**, I mean the culture of American consumerism, driven by expanding media, communication, information, manufacturing, and distribution technologies.

By **consumerism**, I mean the belief in and support of a "social and economic order that encourages people to buy goods and services beyond what they need for survival or to display status. In economics, consumerism is the theory that consumer spending is the main driver of economic growth and a key measure of a capitalist economy's success."[1] Consumerism also includes the notion that people's well-being and happiness depend on obtaining consumer goods and material possessions.

* * * * *

Readers will quickly notice that the ideas of Karl Marx and a host of more recent so-called Neo-Marxist thinkers appear frequently in this book. This

---

[1] Peter N. Stearns, *Consumerism in World History: The Global Transformation of Desire* (New York And London; Routledge, 2006).

1

might cause some to conclude that this is a Marxist or a communist work. It is not. As the book clearly points out, history has proved Marx wrong on many counts. Focusing primarily on production, he failed to fully grasp the future power and the self-preserving complexity of the consumption side of the Capitalist economic equation, although he did insightfully observe that commodities in the marketplace seem to possess certain mystical qualities.

However magical the marketplace might have become and however successful modern capitalism might appear, it is abundantly clear that, in the Late Modern Era, our capitalist economic engine is not without its faults, oversights, and abuses. Social and economic inequity, racism, xenophobia, and environmental plunder too often go unaddressed in a self-perpetuating system that continually seeks to conceal its true nature. In this context, many of the critiques of capitalism offered by Marx and his followers have proved extraordinarily useful. The aim of this book is not to overthrow capitalism, but to perfect it by exposing its shortcomings and its well-oiled masking mechanisms.

CHAPTER ONE: PRISONERS OF CONSUMERISM

The King of Prussia

In 1961 in suburban Philadelphia, construction began on the world's first great shopping mall, the King of Prussia. In that same year, "Walt Disney's Wonderful World of Color" aired its first program and triggered the future success of color television. Although at the time, these two seemingly unconnected and little-remembered events appeared to be routine steps in the ongoing march of American architectural and technological progress, they in fact constituted a cultural watershed of sorts, offering us a tantalizing peak into the blindingly vibrant future of the nation's emerging consumer culture.

American consumer culture is the child of American consumerism, and it has been a long time coming. We can find hints of its infancy in the marketplaces of old, and we can trace its long adolescence from the first European shopping arcades, department stores, and trade expositions of the nineteenth century to the appearance of American "strip-mall" shopping centers and amusement parks in the twentieth. Like so many other voices within the current popular culture, today's consumer culture also has roots in the development of photography and the printed image, in early radio, sound recording, and in the flat, live, documentary broadcasts of early black-and-white TV. However, it was not until the spectacle of the modern mall and box-store revolutionized the contemporary American shopping experience and the saturation of color propelled American television into the present dream-world of fantasy and illusion that the mature culture of American consumerism was born.

The history of the King of Prussia mall mirrors the brief history of mature American consumer culture. Completed in 1963, the project turned the traditional strip-mall inside out. Instead of focusing outwardly on the parking lot, the street, and the world beyond, this new kind of mall focused inwardly on a dazzling central plaza that featured a spectacle of architectural amenities including fountains, elaborate landscaping, gazebos, and an eight-sided amphitheater. By 1967, it had grown to include three enormous department stores, Gimbels, JCPenney, and Wanamaker, and much of the central mall area had been enclosed to create elaborate passageways and grand glassed-in atriums. By this time, it incorporated over 1,300,000 square feet of store space occupied by over 140 stores. The subsequent addition of "fashion-oriented" retailers like Bloomingdale's, Nieman Marcus, Lord & Taylor, and Nordstrom shifted the retail focus upscale. By the first decade of the 21st century, the King of Prussia enclosed over 3,000,000 square feet and was home to seven department stores, 365 specialty shops and 40 restaurants, all surrounded by fountains, enormous live indoor plantings including indoor trees, clearstory skylights, glittering food courts, Italian marble flooring, stained glass windows, and an ever-changing circus of amusements, distractions, curiosities, and entertainments. All over the country similar malls sprang up, and shopping began to be associated with elaborate entertainments like those featured at the 4,200,000 square foot Mall of America, which opened in suburban Minneapolis in 1992 featuring 520 shops, 14 movie screens, numerous concert venues, an underground aquarium, and an indoor family amusement park. A new cultural force was at work, and the central focus of modern life was shifting.

Meanwhile, the 1961 debut and subsequent popularity of "Walt Disney's Wonderful World of Color" caused the sale of color TV sets to skyrocket and ushered in a new age of television. In this new age, television was to slowly replace grey documentaries of the word with vibrant fantasies of the image, slowly shifting its focus from the real to the unreal, from a live, evidential form to a manipulated, symbolic form. Early television had been live, and even after the advent of videotape, the medium had retained its live focus, primarily basing its presentations on the knowledge that it was the only medium capable of broadcasting simultaneous visual and audio representations of actual events in real time. However, with the coming of color, the focus of television began to shift from a flat, factual, word-based perspective to a highly aesthetic, visual, image-based perspective centered on the stunning manipulations of images and characterized by graphic overlay, gleaming collage, replays, special effects, and all manner of fantastic technical manipulations.[2] This was not simply a change in the "look" of television; this was a dramatic shift in the very nature of television itself. The medium was changing its content, shifting its fundamental meanings. TV had begun as a medium of the believable, a real-life representation of entertainments and events. In 1961, it began its short journey toward becoming a medium of art-directed fantasy, manipulation, and illusion: consumerism's perfect messenger.

By 1961, it appeared that many traditional American institutions—work, family, church, school—were crumbling. Meanwhile, invisibly, insidiously, a rapidly emerging consumer culture was busy creating new institutions to fill the void: leisure, consumption, celebrity—all draped in entertainments of the most fantastic sort. Since 1961, leisure, not work, has been the venue in which we define ourselves, and shopping and watching TV have come to define that leisure. Today, for most, work is no longer the central focus of American life, and shopping is no longer a utilitarian necessity. The mall is no longer merely a place to shop for the things we need; it has become a place to be, a place to express ourselves and to satisfy our desires. Television is no longer a source of information and a novel diversion; it has taken possession of our very souls. Without ever sensing the presence of its confining walls, we have become willing prisoners lost in the enticing folds of consumerism's blinding hall of mirrors.

Prisoners of Consumerism

Today in America, we are seduced. Tenderly ensnared in a sparkling web so enticing, we perceive no reason to struggle. Unwitting captives in gleaming prisons so inviting, so intoxicating, we are blinded by their dazzling glow, and we fail to recognize the bars. Slowly, inexorably, insidiously we have become docile, even willing slaves, anesthetized by the popular culture and the all-encompassing enormity of spectacles and fascinations that today engulf our world. Critics warn that, while it appears to constitute reality, today's popular culture in fact destroys the real and replaces it with illusion, fantasy, and exhilarating simulations; the depthless dream worlds it has taught us to crave, the well-appointed, labyrinthine dungeons it has taught us to love.

The past half-century has seen enormous material progress in the West, and we have witnessed an unprecedented upward spiral in the standard of living. By the turn of the last century, the average American was consuming

---

[2] John Caldwell, *Televisuality: Style, Crisis, and Authority in American Television* (New Brunswick, NJ: Rutgers University Press, 1995).

twice as many goods and services as in 1950, and the average home built at that time was twice as large as those erected in the post war era. In fact, as one scholar so informally puts it, "Most of the world most of the time spends most of its energy producing and consuming more and more stuff." [3] Certainly, most of us would agree that this is a good thing. Nonetheless, we have come to define ourselves in our "stuff," create ourselves through things, and change ourselves by changing our things. Whether or not this is a good thing is a question for debate. There are those who warn that, in our unbridled materialism, we are often unaware of the ways in which our notions of what constitutes progress have been manipulated, unaware of what a free and uncontrolled life and a wholesome standard of living might actually be.

Despite the recent collapse of world communism, Marx was right in a few disturbingly ironic ways. Today there is still a "specter haunting Europe," but it is not the specter of communist revolution that Marx predicted. It is the onrushing specter of advancing world capitalism that communism opposed, an apparition that has proved a great deal more resilient, more robust, and more all-embracingly powerful than anything Marx and Engels predicted. And it haunts not just Europe, American, and the West; it now is commencing to haunt the entire world. When Marx mused, "all that is solid melts into air," he was suggesting that, as capitalism "constantly revolutionizes" the technological "instruments of production," it sweeps away established social relations in the process[4]—that consumer goods and their means of production are actually agents of social control. Well, consumer capitalism may have indeed swept away most of those "fixed, fast-frozen relations" and a great deal more in the bargain. Nevertheless, and despite its unfettered, exploitative, alienating power, "capitalist production" did not "beget its own negation" as Marx anticipated.[5] Capitalism did not contain the seeds of its own destruction. Quite the contrary, it appears to have given birth to its own irreversible, self-perpetuating, regeneration. Today, employing methods far more fantastic than anything that Marx could have dreamed, consumer capitalism invisibly accomplishes this unexpected miracle of domination by way of gossamer, all-engrossing, cultural phenomena created by runaway consumerism. It is the aim of this book to define consumer culture, to

---

[3] James Twitchell, "Two Cheers for Materialism" in Juliet B. Schor and Douglas B. Holt ed., *The Consumer Society Reader* (New York: The New Press, 2000), 281.

[4] Karl Marx and Friedrich Engels, *Manifesto of the Communist Party*, trans. Samuel Moore, in Robert C. Tucker, ed. *The Marx-Engels Reader*, 2nd edition (New York: Norton, 1978), 473-83.

[5] Karl Marx, Capital, *The Communist Manifesto and Other Writings*, ed. Julian Borchardt (New York: The Modern Library, 1932), 199.

unmask its complex, uncharted workings—visible and invisible, miraculous and insidious, freeing and enslaving—and to suggest, paraphrasing Marx, that the workers of today's world—meaning all of us—may have invisible chains of a very different sort to lose.

When illuminated by the neon light of today's consumer culture, Marx's miscalculations appear obvious. As it turns out, it is not the workers of the world who must unite in revolution against the inevitable tyranny of capitalist exploitation that Marx observed in 1848. Today the emphasis has shifted to the other side of the equation. Today many scholars suspect that a very different kind of oppression flows not from work but from leisure, not from production but from consumption, resulting not in polarized class struggle but in the manipulation of human identities. The chains that are said to bind us today are not those of the exploitation of the worker, but those of the seduction of the consumer. According to this critique, our consumer culture homogenizes class and enslaves its victims, not with the iron fist of industrial exploitation, but with the countless gossamer threads of marketing, image, internet, and media—translucent seductions that bind us to gleaming leisure-time fabrications of dream-like perfection.

While it is true that Marx put forward certain theories regarding "consumer fetishism" in the very first chapter of *Das Kapital*, and that he undoubtedly glimpsed some dim shadow of the future, Marxian visions of "use value" and the "social character of labor" and of the masking effects of the "exchange value" of commodities described only the tip of the commodity iceberg. Similarly, subsequent insights into the mysterious effects of conspicuous consumption and theories regarding the seductions and manipulative workings of the early, so-called "culture industry," although prophetic, are about as far from the present staggeringly multifarious operations of the popular culture, as early radio broadcasts are from MTV.

In a disturbingly ironic way, Marx was right about the mystical nature of commodities in the marketplace. He just wasn't right enough. His critique of bourgeois capitalism turned on an imbalance that masked the overt exploitation of the workers and foreshadowed the class struggles he was sure would follow. Although he knew that capitalism possessed the substantial ability to blind and control the hapless proletariat and to perpetuate its own dominant ideology, he was certain that this "false consciousness," as the blinding and controlling mechanisms were later termed, was not permanent. He was sure that the masses would eventually recognize their plight and rise up in revolution. About this he could not have been more wrong. In his wildest dreams, Marx could not have imagined the vitality and complexity of the mechanisms by which modern consumer culture would come to subdue and control, not just the workers, but society as a whole. He could never have foreseen that the system's methods would become so diverse, so flexible, so imaginative, so elastic, so responsive to every criticism, to every negative critique in his precious dialectic. Unsuspected by Marx, capitalism's ability to mask its true grasping, self-cloning nature was so opaque, so economically and politically adroit, so seemingly accommodating to every objection, that today it begins to appear that there is no worthy negative side of the dialectic left to continue the battle. Whether this is a good thing or a bad thing is one of the subjects of this book.

To be sure, Americans have not come to embrace this life of getting and spending against their better judgment; they have demanded such a life. Still, the question remains as to whether our judgment has been manipulated and whether our embrace of the world of the commodity leads to powerlessness or to liberation.

Analysis by Example

So how do we best systematically explore the glitzy, superficial, depthless world of contemporary American consumer culture? Like many who ponder such things, I have found that cultural phenomena are often best articulated and most easily explored through the use of examples. Many of today's finest minds have exhausted considerable effort to illustrate the allure of consumer culture by citing examples of its workings. In this literature, Disneyland and Las Vegas are perhaps the most often ⁓used metaphors. These constitute both accurate and unfortunate selections. They are accurate because these artificial fantasy worlds epitomize the ability of the agents of American materialism to produce enticing spectacles, completely control enormous numbers of spectators, weave elaborate dreamlike webs of fantasy, and, in short, suspend reality. In fact, the word "Disneyfication" has been coined to describe the construction of these all-too-perfect artificial fabrications. Places like the reproduction of Jamestown and Williamsburg in Virginia and the built-from-scratch duplication of the cave and the ancient cave paintings at Lascaux II in Southern France come immediately to mind, but such phenomena extend everywhere—to planned communities, shopping arcades, amusement parks, and to a whole range of contemporary architectural and commercial output.

As useful as these grand examples might be in illustrating the disorienting nature of today's popular culture, they are also unfortunate in that they tend to obscure its pervasive, everyday character. By focusing on its most spectacular creations, one tends to ignore its endless array of lesser manifestations and to lose sight of all the tiny nodes of contact that control us on a daily basis. Every ad, every image, every seductive utterance has weight, and the massive preponderance of these unrelenting mini-assaults has passed the point where it can be quantified, repulsed, or even identified. The complex workings of this culture of consumption have become a seemingly natural part of our everyday life and are thus no longer a part of our conscious awareness.

And so, it seems natural enough for me, as one who is prone to contemplate these things, to offer readers examples to help unmask this hidden cultural machinery. Like most similes, these are not without their problems. At one time, I used the term "The Gloss" to collectively refer to the myriad manifestations of consumer culture. Certainly, "The Gloss" is an apt enough term to describe the gleaming artificial commercial sheen that covers the Western World, but contrary to the connotation of "glossy-ness," the Gloss is not a hard, impenetrable veneer. It is rather a fluid, viscous coating that sucks us in and holds us suspended in its oozing neon allure. It is an amorphous, shape-shifting, infinitely elastic, mesmerizing pool that ensnares and fascinates us, while at the same time, it remains elusive, ingrained, taken for granted, and thus largely unnoticed. In The Gloss, as the name implies, our attention is focused on an array of gleaming reflections, and so we are unable to see the vast, multifaceted phenomenon as a whole. Immersed and atomized, we remain largely unaware of our own immersion and blind to the plight of those around us.

By whatever name, agents of our consumer culture operate all around us. As the numbing waters that they disperse enfold us, we surrender both to their high-end splendor and to their seedy underbellies of honky-tonks and dives. Fascinated by mesmerizing spectacles and seduced by anesthetizing persuasions, we find their power everywhere: department stores and malls with their intoxicating allures, fast-food restaurants, seedy dives and greasy-spoons, every theater, every TV set, computer monitor, sports arena, shabby strip-mall, grocery, convenience store, signboard, display window, skyscraper, warehouse, newspaper, photograph—all are nodes of a vast, interconnected web of brainwashing seduction and manipulative illusion. Although wondrous in character and seemingly countless in number, the choices presented all seem to point in the same direction—inward, back toward the perpetuation and growth of the system. Even though today rapidly accelerating change appears to be the hallmark of culture, changes in consumption habits appear to be allowed only in directions desired by the system.

It is the theme of this book that American consumer culture and all its ongoing, numbing manipulations have been recently perfected in the intricate workings of a vast and fantastic illusion of choice, employing breathtaking fireworks of all colors, shapes, and forms. Are these illusions so enticing as to have effectively muted any possible revolutionary outcry? Have they silenced the historically predictable anthem of the exploited and hidden from them the fact of their own exploitation? Have they sated any desire aimed at breaking the chains of this material bondage? Does the popular culture effectively mask widespread inequity, poverty, powerlessness, even murder and genocide? Are we inexorably overwhelmed by its irresistible power to intoxicate, to seduce, to stupefy? Are we willing slaves to an invisible force that shapes our beliefs and our desires and blinds us to its own workings while it obscures the unmistakable stains of human bondage that surround us daily? Or does our consumer culture have another side? Does it ensure a healthy economy and foster growth and well-being? Does it spawn unforeseen meanings and supply important material and symbolic resources that ordinary people can use to construct their lives, their identities, and their culture?

With these questions in mind, let us now examine a few specific examples of consumer culture at work. I selected these three examples, more or less at random, by driving around in a popular commercial area north of Atlanta, where within the radius of a mile or so one encounters hundreds of shops, service outlets, stores, and restaurants, including Abercrombie and Fitch, Ann Taylor, BrandsMart, Brookstone, the Sports Authority, the Disney Store, Express, Foot Locker, Fredericks of Hollywood, Hobby World, McDonald's, Target, the Body Shop, the Cracker Barrel, Wendy's, and hundreds more. From these possible examples, I have somewhat arbitrarily selected three: The Cracker Barrel, McDonald's, and a regional discount retail appliance outlet called BrandsMart.

Cracker Barrel

Let us begin our investigation by exploring one of a chain of American roadside restaurants called The Cracker Barrel Old Country Store and Restaurant. At this writing, 662 of these establishments serve customers along interstate highways in 45 states. They are essentially all the same. All serve the same menu, sport generally the same décor and decoration, and sell the exact same items in the gift shop. All are identically arranged. Each store is a clone, a simulacrum, an exact copy, not of some real, original country-store prototype, but of a fiction, an ideal. Each purveys a carefully fabricated, imagined image, a wildly superficial rendering of what a rustic, American country store of an earlier era might look like in the present age of plastic flowers and manufactured antiques. Once inside these massive, windowless structures, one is hard -pressed to tell whether it is in Georgia or California, whether it is now or last week or thirty years ago. Thus, we immediately see here two important characteristics of the working of consumer culture: the endless production and reproduction of copies of copies for which there is no original, and the orchestrated manipulation and displacement of space and time.

One enters Cracker Barrel by passing along a reproduction of a long, rustic front porch decorated with weathered old signs and lined with newly manufactured facsimiles of old wooden rocking chairs, all shaded by a shed roof. The effect might at first appear inviting, but for those who pause to take a seat in one of the caned rockers, it quickly becomes clear that the porch offers only a view of the parking lot that surrounds the building and that the rockers all sport price tags and are for sale. What does not become immediately clear is the operation of a particular aspect of America's consumer culture, which is manifest in the fact that it is not rockers that Cracker Barrel is *really* selling here, nor is it the "country style" meals served inside, nor the rusticated new items in the well-stocked "country store" style gift shop. The gleaming commodity that this successful roadside chain *really* has for sale is illusion, symbol, cultural association. At the bottom of it all, the Cracker Barrel Old Country Store and Restaurant is a purveyor of nostalgia. This successful chain thrives on the sale of largely inaccurate, gleaming distortions of the past. The products in the gift shop, the décor in the dining area, even the food itself all combine to create a carefully manufactured dreamlike vision of Americana, bathed in contrived patriotism and the perceived goodness of a simple country life that is no more.

Entering the building from the rambling porch, one enters the Cracker Barrel Shop, a veritable theme park of ambiance and atmosphere featuring intimate displays of carefully selected product lines, all aimed at summoning up half-remembered associations with a not-too-distant, patriotic past. These products all cater to the contemporary consumer's insatiable drive for novelty. Unlike its alleged model, the American country store of an earlier era, which featured orderly rows of floor-to-ceiling shelves filled with the utilitarian necessities of everyday life, the Cracker Barrel Shop features chaotic arrays of frivolous merchandise aimed at the lowest common denominator. Wandering through this kaleidoscopic playscape-allegory of glitz, the manipulation of patriotic and nostalgic signs is everywhere: in the "Simple Heart Canister Set," featuring three ceramic kitchen canisters, a farmhouse, a barn, and a church, labeled "family," "freedom," and "faith," respectively; in "the Farm Couple Salt and Pepper Set," featuring a miniature farmer and farm wife holding a pitchfork and flower basket; in the "Flying Angel Night Light" in the design of a winged angel wearing a red and white striped apron and a starry blue cape. There is a whole line of products decorated with an "Apple Blossom" motif, including bowls, birdhouses, plates, mugs, and pot holders inscribed "Home Sweet Home." There is also a plug-in electric "Home Fragrancer" guaranteed to fill your house with the "fresh from the orchard" aroma of McIntosh apples. Reciting the banal dreams of mass consumption, the hand-picked inventory goes on and on in this bizarre emporium of mass-produced merchandise aimed at creating an unstable hallucination of the past, a superficial mélange of contrived Americana and paper-thin, rubber-stamp values.

Passing through the shop, one enters the dining area, an ample open space filled with lacquered knotty-pine tables and surrounded by walls copiously adorned with antique farm implements, kitchen utensils, tools, and other rustic memorabilia, along with photographs, signage, and advertising from the early part of the last century. In the current parlance of consumerism, these are "collectibles," that is to say, commodified "relics," old everyday items and junk transformed into valuable icons of America's rural past. Their perceived value does not flow so much from their scarcity, their uniqueness, nor from their former utility, as it does from their camp, emblematic ability to recall "the good ol' days" of the once-ubiquitous family farm, that sacred, iconic source of all that is perceived to be good and wholesome in America.

As one might expect, the menu also conforms to these nostalgic themes. Here one finds traditional "American" favorites like country fried chicken, meatloaf, country fried steak, chicken and dumplings, and fried pork chops. There is also an array of breakfast selections (served anytime) including meal combinations described as "Country Boy," "Smokehouse," and "Country Morning," all comprised of grits, "sawmill" gravy, buttermilk biscuits, country ham, and the like.

So it is that everything at the Cracker Barrel County Store and Restaurant is designed to contribute to a carefully orchestrated spectacle of display, nostalgia, and nationalism in a contrived dreamscape of intensified representation that is cut off from the outside world and precariously suspended in space and time. The result is a glowing distillation of the twice-removed "old country store" reality upon which it is all symbolically modeled, a place where consumption involves an obvious manipulation of signs, a manipulation that subtly effaces the distinction between image and reality. At the Cracker Barrel, in an effort to entice, fascinate, and mystify the hungry consumer, the past and the present seem to switch places and thus distort our ongoing perception of both.

McDonald's

My sister once joked that she thought that the very first word her young son ever uttered was "McDonald's." Like most jokes this one has grounding in truth. The image of parents forcibly pulled by their kids into the carefully constructed McFantasy world of fries, burgers and chicken McNuggets is familiar to most Americans. Over the years, the great empire that lies beneath the Golden Arches has penetrated deep into the very soul of American culture and consciousness, and the fast-food giant is now hard at work burrowing its way into other cultures all around the world. One might dare to speculate that at the end of it all there may one day be a new McWorld with its own McCulture.

A great deal has been written in the last twenty years about "McDonaldization" as an economic paradigm, a social force, and an agent of globalization. Most of this critique focuses on the enormous fast-food chain as an agent of modern woes, that is, on the ongoing homogenization, massification, and standardization that the "McDonald's phenomenon" has deployed "to dominate more and more sectors of American society as well as the rest of the world."[6] With its Golden Arches, Ronald McDonalds, and saturation media advertising, few contemporary institutions are as well known as McDonald's, and few have contributed more to the development of modern systems aimed at "increased efficiency, calculability, predictability, and control." Indeed, the corporation's "rationalization," organization, and control of both "production and consumption...is unparalleled in the contemporary era."[7] However, there is a great deal more to McDonald's corporate control mechanisms than cold, economic and social manipulations; there is a mystical, ethereal, uniquely cultural side to the fast-food giant's self-serving ability to shape our desires, needs, and perceptions. In short, McDonald's is a mega-agent of today's consumer culture.

Operating 40,000 restaurants worldwide, the fast-food giant serves a staggering 69 million customers each day, and as one might expect, McDonald's sweeping manipulations within the popular culture constitute an all-embracing reflection of the company's size, power, and image-building

---

[6] George Ritzer, *The McDonaldization of Society*, Second Edition (Thousand Oaks, CA: Pine Forge Press, 1996), 1.
[7] Douglas Kellner, "Theorizing/Resisting McDonaldization: A Multiperspective Approach," at "Illuminations: The Critical Theory Website," http://www.uta.edu/illuminations/Kell30.htm.

expertise. In displays, promotional tie-ins with popular films, toy giveaways, charity operations, and saturation advertising, the illusions purveyed by this vast, global burger-empire are among the most penetrating found anywhere. McDonald's does not seek simply to alter our perception of the world around us; McDonald's seeks to alter our perception of ourselves. Management makes no apology for these manipulations. The corporation's Annual Report puts it nicely, "When customers enter one of our stores, they enter our Brand."[8] The "McDonald's Brand" is the corporation's carefully refined and attractively packaged distillation of cultural manipulation and imagery as experienced either directly in the restaurant or via myriad media points of entry. Propelled by fantasies of family, ethnicity, nationality, charity, modernity, and fun, McDonald's promises to magically reward each customer or potential customer with the illusion of a new and improved lifestyle, and a better, hipper, more engaged self.

Such sweeping transformations take on ideological significance. In "Theorizing/Resisting McDonaldization," Douglas Kellner sums it up:

> McDonaldization is thus an ideology as well as a set of social practices, a cultural construct with its myths, semiotic codes, and discourses. McDonald's itself projects an ideology of the U.S. as a melting pot in which all citizens participate equally in its democratic pleasures, irregardless [sic] of race, class, gender, and age. It furnishes a model of the United States as a land of consumer innovation and technical rationality which produces inexpensive and desirable goods for all, serving its customer's needs and providing a valuable product. McDonald's associates itself with traditions like the family, national holidays, patriotism, Christian charity, and the icons of media culture. Going to McDonald's is thus joining the consumer society, partici- pating in the national culture, and validating common values.[9]

When we enter McDonald's, we consume symbolic values and illusions. In a postmodern miracle of transubstantiation, burgers and fries are transformed into family fun, American know-how and expertise, and all the perceived goodness and convenience of modernity itself. When we bite into a Big Mac, we are enticed to accept the promise that, through the products we consume, we can change our lifestyle and alter who we are.

The term lifestyle is very much in vogue these days. In contemporary consumer culture the term "lifestyle" is linked to one's "individuality, self- expression, and stylistic self-conscientiousness." One's home, car, clothes, leisure pastimes, eating and drinking preferences, and so on, are perceived

---

[8] McDonald's Corporation, *2006 Annual Report*, http://www.McDonalds.com/corp/invest/ pub/2006_Annual_Report.html
[9] Douglas Kellner, "Theorizing/Resisting McDonaldization."

to reflect one's "individuality of taste and sense of style."[10] Certainly a great deal of these fabricated lifestyle perceptions are created and then reinforced in the contemporary electronic media. McDonald's TV ads not only point to a vast array of illusory choices through which we might "stylize our lives," they also press the central cultural issue of lifestyle fabrication into the foreground. We are constantly reminded that we speak not only with our clothes, our cars, and all our other possessions, we also fabricate and display our personal styles through the food we consume. For kids, McDonald's seeks to represent a life of fun; for middle America, it presents a perception of a road to a wholesome family life of bonding and togetherness; for urban black America, "Mickey-Dee's" attempts to put forward an illusion of trend and of ethnic unity. For everyone, these ads seek to create the unambiguous notion that eating at McDonald's makes one a part of the modern scene, enjoying modern pleasures, taking advantage of modern speed, efficiency, and know-how, reaping the benefits of modern progress, and living an efficient, modern lifestyle.

Just as Cracker Barrel creates controlled illusions of the past, McDonald's creates controlled illusions of the present, a fantasy world in which benevolent technology is harnessed in a well-oiled, modern carnival of fun. Beneath the Golden Arches one finds a vibrant circus-like vision of modernity that is a far cry from the grey, plodding, conformist, mass culture predicted by so many earlier critics of the modern age. This illusion of carnival, circus, festival, and fair is no coincidence. The desired illusion may be modern efficiency, predictability, and convenience, but in a contradictory reversal that is typical of consumer culture's invisible manipulations, upbeat modern dreams are magically fabricated in the murky depths of our historical consciousness. Ancient cultural memories of the carnivalesque are subtly appropriated and intensified. The result is a controlled midway of fascination and calculated seduction.

This kind of control is today familiar throughout the fast-food industry where the perfection of "things such as replicated settings, scripted interactions with customers, predictable employee behavior, and predictable products,"[11] are universally employed to "control" and "exploit" consumers, leading customers to a kind of "rationalized re-enchantment." At McDonald's, the rainbow-like Golden Arches themselves suggest something magical and occult. Beneath their alluring sweep we find multicolored enclosed playscapes for kids, gleaming sideshow-like signage announcing an

---

[10] Mike Featherstone, *Consumer Culture and Postmodernism* (London and Thousand Oaks, CA: SAGE Publications, 1991), 83.

[11] George, Ritzer, *Enchanting a Disenchanted World: Revolutionizing the Means of Consumption* (London: Pine Forge Press, 1999), 84-85.

array of fried and grilled midway treats, as well as up-to-date kewpie doll toy giveaways and fun house promotions. All this consumption-inducing activity takes place in a well-lit big top dominated by circus-like reds and yellows and presided over by Ronald McDonald, the fast-food chain's central icon, who directs a multi-ring circus of Happy Meals, charitable organizations, and media tie-ins that flaunt the biggest stars of sport, film, and television. While Ronald poses with Michael Jordan, Shrek, or R2D2, we recall from earlier television ads that he lives in an Oz-like land where the flowers talk and "freak-show" characters like Mayor McCheese and the "Hamburgerlar" [sic] call up half-forgotten images of the days when the midway offered peepshow glimpses of the exotic and the grotesque, of places where kids were once both fascinated and frightened at the same time and where adults were given permission to act like children.

Although the contrived circus at McDonald's does not turn on the same kind of blatant nostalgia offered up at Cracker Barrel, it nonetheless creates a backward glance that is uniquely its own. This is not the nostalgia of the broad American entrepreneurial epic but an inwardly turned fascination with the early days of McDonald's itself as a historical part of the American cultural experience. Quite rightly, McDonald's sees itself as part of America's cultural tradition, as the originator of the fast-food industry, as a pioneer in the perfection of mass production, mass promotion, and mass consumption techniques, indeed, as one of the inventors of consumer culture itself. The corporation would have us all look back on its own past and behold a reflection of the American Dream: the Horatio Alger story of Ray Kroc and "the little company that could," the first restaurants with their fifteen-cent hamburgers, the growth of the Brand, the image, the institution. To this end, McDonald's has built a museum of its own history and remodeled select stores in the image of one of its early stores from the 1950s, thus creating a campy cult of McDonald's memorabilia. Collectors have sprung up everywhere, and the market for old McDonald's giveaway items is enormous. In a plastic landslide of free cups and plates and action figures, hundreds of past promotional toy and trinket giveaways —created to induce the consumption of commodities—have become commodities themselves. Consumerism commodifies everything, even its own commodification of everything. In the process, a new aesthetic appears that destroys the distinction between the blossoming art of popular culture and traditional high art forms. What was once a cheap child's toy becomes an iconic "collectible." The mundane, the mass produced, and the everyday become confused with objects of art; and finally, in another of the consumer culture's remarkable transformations, what was once banal is rendered fantastic[12] as a component of the popular culture renders such items "camp," turning yesterday's trash into art itself.

Thus, in many ways, McDonald's reaches out to heighten and expand its circus of illusions, resurrecting the ghost of the carnival, embracing its own past, and forging ties to other areas within the popular culture itself. Clowns, plastic cups, rock icons, film stars, and sports heroes all take their place beneath the Golden Arches. But at McDonald's, as elsewhere, things are never what they seem. Our consumer culture creates a glowing gossamer veil that hides the real operation of the modern world. The reality is that McDonald's has redefined many aspects of modern life including our perception of "diet and culinary value, familial togetherness, and communal experience," replacing home-prepared food with commodified food, and displacing, if not destroying, traditional family eating practices.[13] Distracted by the synthesized signs of modernity and a carnivalesque atmosphere of fun, fantasy, and illusion, customers at McDonald's participate in a scientifically controlled and yet seemingly chaotic festival of images that totally masks the cold, ploddingly methodical, industrial production and consumption of mass-produced food.

All this notwithstanding, the McDonaldization of the world is not proceeding along the totalitarian, industrialized, homogenizing lines that many critics had predicted. The alchemy of the fast-food giant may be built around the implied promise of a modern lifestyle, but the fantasies that abound beneath the Golden Arches offer a great deal more than just a single, cookie-cutter image of life in the new age. Like all agents of popular culture, McDonald's and the other mushrooming fast-food chains offer consumers a complex variety of choices attached to an equally complex variety of signs and symbolic illusions. From this fabulous smorgasbord, you can fashion your modern self after a vast assortment of lifestyle models. You can "mix and match," or as one competitor puts it so aptly, you can "have it your way." McDonald's is not just a monotony of burgers: there are McSalads and McFish, McChicken and McRibs. Each morning the Sausage McGriddle takes its place alongside the Egg McMuffin. Although we were told the modern age would be about uniformity, conformity, monotony, and the grey drudgery of mechanization, today at McDonald's we are offered seemingly endless color and variety.

This variety is particularly evident when we look at McDonald's as an agent of globalization. Those same critics, who saw the modern age as an age

---

[12] Susan Sontag, "Notes on Camp," in *Against Interpretation* (New York: Farrar, Straus & Giroux, 1966).

[13] Douglas Kellner, "Theorizing/Resisting McDonaldization."

of uniformity and repetitive toil, viewed globalization as a dehumanizing, homogenizing force. When first coined, the term McDonaldization suggested a synthesizing and conforming Americanization of the world. Clearly, this definition has turned out to be well off the mark because it did not anticipate the workings of modern consumerism. Although first seen as a purveyor of up-to-date mechanized efficiencies and shallow American popular culture, on the global stage McDonald's has proved surprisingly flexible, adapting to local conditions everywhere. In India, the Maharajah Mac is made with mutton. In Israel, Big Macs are sold without cheese to avoid conflicting with kosher traditions requiring the separation of meat and dairy products. Spaniards enjoy the McPepito, a tasty veal sandwich fashioned after a traditional Iberian favorite. In Germany, Würstel and beer are sold under the Golden Arches, while Norwegian patrons order salmon sandwiches, and so on.

Somewhere in all this diversity, there is certainly an Americanizing influence; and to be sure McDonald's still represents a monolithic, modern, homogenizing force aimed at numbing conformity. Nonetheless, the clear emphasis here is not only on Americanization and modern efficiencies, but also on diversity, difference, variety, and choice. Here we see the adaptive flexibility of consumerism. McDonaldization worldwide is not simply a vast, standardized, rigid mold designed to stamp out clones of modern American life. Indeed, as time passes, McDonaldization seems readily adaptable to local cultures and remarkably fluid in its acquiescence to demands for a healthier menu. Accordingly, the spectrum of lifestyle associations that the global chain now offers constitutes a vast, fluid assortment of blended, cultural components in constant motion, symbols not only of American conformity but also of substantial cultural variety and difference. Popular culture may anesthetize us, seduce us, even enslave us, but it is not always a homogenizing force. Even though at its heart, it seeks its own replication and reproduction, today's consumer culture seeks to seduce us with a fantastic array of choices, appearing to celebrate novelty and to abhor conformity.

BrandsMart

BrandsMart is a small chain of discount home appliance and electronics retailers operating eleven enormous stores in Georgia and Florida. A visit to one of these locations supplies a vivid example of the vast and varied cornucopia of choices presented to us in today's sprawling consumer world. Indeed, at BrandsMart, the spectacle of consumer culture *is* variety.

Entering the large brick, block, and steel, warehouse-like BrandsMart store through the small, restricted entrance, we find ourselves suddenly dwarfed by a cavernous interior that immediately challenges our capacity for assimilation with a single, breathtaking panorama of virtually everything the store has to offer. The effect is disorienting. The outside world quickly disappears as a multi-level fantasylandscape of goods for sale spreads out before our eyes, dominates our consciousness, and focuses our attention on the vast spectacle of the commodity. Below, small appliances, toasters and blenders and microwaves, abound in profusion; around the perimeter, electronics, TVs and stereos and computers dance in seemingly endless variety; and above on the surrounding mezzanine, washers and dryers and ranges and refrigerators and dishwashers of every possible description dominate the scene. Luminescent lime-green, shocking magenta, and international orange banners announce "Washers," "DVD Players," and "Toaster Ovens" in garish disregard for conventional taste and aesthetics. Nonetheless, there is an aesthetic at work here, the blended, base, neon, in-your-face aesthetic so often employed by the popular culture. Cut off from the outside world by a fantasyinterior that seems to have no outside, and that isolates us from conventional notions of beauty, logic, and order, we enter the frantic, dream-like world of consumption where it is our privilege to view the genie in its bottle. We are confused and yet at the same time strangely overwhelmed by an unexplainable urge to buy something. As one customer put it, "This store scares me, yet intrigues me at the same time. It's a big circular pit, filled with a fantastic selection of all sorts of merchandise for the home. Still, I like it because it's a trip into another world."[14]

Everywhere at BrandsMart, the tyranny of the brand assaults us: Hotpoint, Maytag, GE, Amana, Sony, Panasonic, Frigidaire, Whirlpool, HP, Tappan, KitchenAid. The selection is so vast as to defy any logical process of evaluation and elimination. We find that General Electric makes thirty-five different washing machine models, Maytag, twenty-three, and so on. Confronted with the confounding size of the washing machine spectacle at BrandsMart, any logical feature-by-feature evaluation of these units seems impossible, much less any reasoned assessment of price, economy, or value. But the spectacle itself supplies us with insights as to which unit best conforms, not only to our perceived need, but also to our perception of ourselves. Our consciousness is suddenly flooded with images gleaned from advertising, marketing, television, the internet, and printads— subtle impulses, vague intuitions, and half-forgotten symbols planted long ago by other nodes of today's consumer culture, a culture that robs us of our reason,

---

[14] Deborah N. "Yelp, Real People, Real Reviews," http://www.yelp.com/biz

and then, in our confusion, supplies us with the media-ingrained logic of the brand.

Brands have been described as "complex bundles of meaning."[15] Over time a brand can become imbued with any number of meanings: meanings relating to gender, lifestyle, time, place, occupation, value, fashion, class, age, and so on. These meanings become part of brand awareness via the operation of any number of vehicles, some having to do with explicit marketing efforts by a brand manager (like advertising, packaging, and promotions) and some having to do with the brand's experience and expression within the culture (like movies, TV shows, magazine articles, trends and fads, word-of-mouth, and the like). All of this works to foster symbolic associations that function in ways that are similar to those set forth in myths in which a symbol might evoke a series of meanings, interpretations, and emotional responses.[16] Sorting through this mythological shadowland of image and illusion, individual consumers embrace brands whose symbols line up with their aspirations, values, agendas, and self-perceptions.

The washing machines at BrandsMart offer compelling examples of the kinds of symbols called up by various brand strategies. Maytag cultivates a nostalgic image of the company's one-hundred-year tradition of reliability and quality by pointing to simple, time-honored methods and to the values of yesteryear. At General Electric, on the other hand, the brand image looks to the future stressing innovation and corporate responsibility for solving the contemporary world's "toughest problems." This is the company that once claimed "progress" as its "most important product," and today it informs us that GE is the seat of "imagination at work." The Hotpoint brand dwells in the present. Here meaning turns on the quality of life. "Our appliances," the company's website informs us, "are designed to give you time for the things that matter in your life, your friends, your family, and yourself." The list goes on, and it becomes clear that the world of the brand constitutes a mythical dream world of image, symbol, and blind faith, a world in which we are indoctrinated into imaginary dogmas of prejudice and predisposition, engaged by fantastic catechisms of aspiration, faith, and loyalty, and blindly converted to ungrounded and yet unshakable beliefs.

BrandsMart and the appliances it sells offer only one example of the power of the brand, a power that is embedded everywhere in America's consumer culture. Through the images incorporated in the myriad brands attached to thousands of products, consumers can fashion a complete self. This imagery

---

[15] Grant McCracken, *Culture and Consumption II: Markets, Meaning and Brand Management* (Bloomington: Indiana University Press, 2005), 179.

[16] Roberta Sassatelli, *Consumer Culture: History, Theory, and Politics* (Los Angeles: SAGE Publications, 2007), 127.

is not limited to sweeping generalizations of personal focus like the past, present, and future-oriented agendas implied by the three corporate giants in the above examples. Brand imagery can be extremely focused. Not only can we appropriate broad lifestyle markers like old-time values, imagination, responsibility, progress, integrity, and family unity. We can tweak our individual self-image in the most particular ways. In the clothes we wear, the foods we eat, the furnishings of our home, even the toothpaste and the deodorant we buy, we can fabricate personal identities that are honed razor-sharp. We can be athletic or bookish, prudent or reckless, sensitive, aristocratic, hip, uncompromising, malleable, kooky, homespun, down-to-earth, outgoing, and so on. For example, one brand of Scotch whiskey adopted the logo of a trout-fishing fly. This, when combined with *New Yorker*-style copy, imparted to consumers the possibility of being both a rugged outdoorsman and a person of refinement, culture, and intellect—a kind of "patrician Marlboro man."[17] The language of the brand is the language of today's consumer culture. This endless lexicon of fabricated illusion offers us not only artificial strategies aimed at rebuilding the individualism and personal sense of identity that the modern age has obliterated, but it also creates the mistaken perception that we can actually logically sort through the overwhelmingly complex spectacle of commodities and arrive at "informed and reasonable" purchasing decisions.

Of course, we cannot; and unbeknownst to us, the commodities that we buy carry with them a great deal more illusion and imagery than that imposed by the brand or by any other manipulations of modern advertising and marketing. As Marx reminds us, the commodity is "a very queer thing, abounding in metaphysical subtleties and theoretical niceties."[18]

---

[17] McCracken, *Culture and Consumption II*, 179.

[18] Karl Marx, *Capital: A Critique of the Political Economy* (Moscow: Progress Publishers, 1977), 1:76.

CHAPTER TWO: A BRIEF HISTORY OF CONSUMER CULTURE

This book seeks to explore contemporary American social and economic forces that operate within the popular culture. This chapter presents an abbreviated historical and intellectual overview designed to lay the groundwork for these explorations.

A Thankfully Brief Discussion of Marxian Commodity Fetishism

For all his far-reaching speculations, Karl Marx only assigned real importance to the material structures of production. He considered cultural structures to be derivative and therefore not worthy of attention. In the Marxist view, the consumer contributed nothing of real value, and whatever early manifestations consumer culture Marx may have observed represented only inconsequential artifacts of the structures of production.

Nonetheless, Marx was perhaps the first to recognize that the commodity manifested something of a mystery. For Marx, it was the production of commodities that set mankind apart from the other creatures of the earth. All animals appropriated what they needed from nature, but only man transformed nature to meet his needs, only man labored to create products. Thus, for Marx, the products of labor were reflections of the very essence of humanity itself, and he defined the value of these products as the value of the social labor required to produce them. Certainly, under capitalism, raw materials and machinery were also necessary for production, but the values of these also reflected the value of the social labor required for their production. Therefore, for Marx, "value had its basis in the concrete social relations of capitalist production and expressed the expenditure of a certain amount of social labor in that production."[19]

The mystery arises when these products of labor become commodities, that is, when they reach the marketplace where the concrete social relations of their production are concealed in dazzling spectacles of display and exchange. Here commodities seem to take on a logic all their own, a logic that concludes that their value emanates from something within the commodity itself and from its relationship to other commodities in the marketplace. Objects that are defined by relationships among men suddenly appear to be defined by relationships among things. In the marketplace, a new commodity value emerges which seems to flow from the intrinsic properties of the commodity itself, a value independent of human determination. The seemingly magical power of the commodity to assume the guise of having value in and of itself is what Marx calls commodity fetishism. Marx calls this new value "commodity exchange value," and in a capitalistic market, he observed that this new fetishized value exceeds the value of the social labor used to produce the commodity. The difference he called surplus value, and, to make a very long story short, surplus value becomes capital used to perpetuate and expand the system. Most importantly, this surplus value also defines the exploitation of the labor used in the production of the commodity. So it is that, for Marx, commodity fetishism obscures the true value and essence of the commodity. As Martyn Lee puts it, commodity fetishism "completely disguises the essential social reality of the production of commodities and makes it generally impossible to penetrate down beneath this appearance and identify the real conditions and social relations from which the commodity emerges."[20] So at last, we arrive at the heart of the matter: the hidden appropriation of surplus value by one group from another, that is to say, the exploitation of one class by another.

And so it happened that, way back in the middle of the nineteenth century, Marx sensed something that inspired the magical potency perceived in all fetishes, something transcendent in the marketplace. In the very first chapter of *Das Kapital*, Marx presents us with his "The Fetishism of Commodities and the Secret Thereof." In this section, he describes the commodity fetish emanating from the point of exchange as "mystical," "mysterious," surrounded by "magic and necromancy," and he cites analogies "from the mist-enveloped regions of the religious world."[21] These mysterious emanations have been the

---

[19] Sassatelli, *Consumer Culture*, 9.

[20] Martyn J. Lee, *Consumer Culture Reborn: The Cultural Politics of Consumption* (Routledge: London and New York, 1993), 14.

[21] Karl Marx, *Capital: A Critique of the Political Economy* (Moscow: Progress Publishers, 1977), 1:76-80.

point of departure for investigations of commodification and consumption ever since.

One of the linchpins of modern notions of Georg Lukács is the idea that "when they function in extensive networks, commodities work to suppress the human rational capacity and appeal instead to the emotions, much as a religious fetish appeals to and organizes an irrational belief structure."[22] As early as 1923, Georg Lukács argued that "the cumulative effect of these networks of fetishized commodities is that of a 'second nature,' an environment so suggestively 'real' that we move through it as if it were given and natural when in fact it is a socioeconomic construct."[23] Walter Benjamin was also among the first to emphasize the powerfully illusory quality of this environment, and he was followed by Max Horkheimer, Theodor Adorno, Herbert Marcuse and the rest of the Frankfurt School. More recently, even the most radical of the postmodernists use Marx's ideas as a springboard to ponder their images of endless reproduction, illusion, and symbol. There can be little question that all these thinkers sensed the presence of a mysterious power in the modern marketplace. In this regard, it can be no coincidence that many of these intellectual pioneers had/have, in one way or another, Marxist or Neo-Marxist leanings.

The Origins of Consumer Culture

Attempts to unearth the origins of our current consumer culture in the marketplaces of antiquity are destined to fail. Examinations of the great bazaars of Mesopotamia, the Agoras of Ancient Greece, the teeming markets of Rome, or the enormous markets and fairs that once flourished in medieval Europe offer limited insight into to the all-engrossing spectacle that today characterizes the contemporary marketplace. The commodities exchanged in these historic hubs of trade were not mass-produced, and they masked little of the social conditions that surrounded their production. Indeed, the local merchandise offered at ancient bazaars, markets, and fairs was generally quite transparent in this regard, usually local products of the land or items whose origins were not too far removed from the vendors themselves or from their families. What is more, most of the goods traded were of a highly utilitarian nature: livestock, produce, tools, homespun textiles, pottery, salt, and the like. To be sure, some luxury goods and exotic products from

---

[22] Michael W. Jennings, "Introduction to Walter Benjamin" in *The Writer of Modern Life: Essays on Charles Baudelaire*, ed. Michael W. Jennings (Cambridge, MA and London: The Belknap Press of Harvard University, 2006), 13.

[23] Georg Lukács, *History and Class Consciousness*, quoted in Jennings, "Introduction to Walter Benjamin" in *The Writer of Modern Life*, 13-4.

distant lands were traded in the great markets of old; but these were for the wealthy few, not for the rank-and-file, and the conditions of these products' production, no matter how oppressive, had no meaning, hidden or otherwise, to the hapless masses who could only eye them longingly. The great fairs of medieval Europe did not work toward the pacification and domination of the masses, nor did they work to accomplish the reproduction or perpetuation of the social or economic systems of the times. Although they may have offered modest spectacles and constituted welcome distractions from the drudgery of medieval life, these great markets did not embody the sweeping power of our modern marketplace. Consumer culture is a modern phenomenon, a product of a modern, industrial world (or as some would have it, a postmodern, post-industrial world). Its insidious seductions can only be accomplished in the rarefied atmosphere of a culture of unbridled commodification fueled by mass production, mass consumption, and mass media.

Even though in earlier eras commodities were never the covert agents of institutional regeneration or control, ancient markets and medieval fairs nonetheless supply us with some of the earliest examples of the allures employed by modern marketers. With their bohemian atmosphere of novelty, curiosity, and lust, the fairs, markets, and carnivals of old often accomplished a kind of suspension of reality, a powerful distraction realized in the use of mesmerizing spectacles and fantastic entertainments. Later, intellectually lumped together under the sweeping umbrella of the so-called "carnivalesque," these sometimes crass, lewd, or even grotesque fascinations were thought to be deeply embedded in our cultural souls. Many scholars suggest that it is the half-remembered presence of these ancient attractions, fixations, and fears, lingering deep within our individual and collective cultural psyche, that today's culture plays upon to accomplish its invisible seductions. This school of thought insists that the tradition of the pre-industrial carnivalesque is still present within today's consumer culture, that the carnivalesque has been recently displaced into media images, design, advertising, rock music, videos, and sites of consumption like holiday resorts, sports arenas, theme parks, department stores, and shopping centers.[24]

Although the medieval fair did not act as a mechanism of social control, it did present the peasantry with emancipating moments. Amid the spectacle and distraction of the great fairs, the common people were perhaps as far away as they would ever get from the strangling yoke of feudal society and from the looming presence of the church. Citing Mikhail Bakhtin,[25] Mike

[24] Featherstone, *Consumer Culture and Postmodernism*, 22.
[25] Mikhail Bakhtin, *Rabelais and his World* (Cambridge, MA: MIT Press, 1968).

Featherstone puts it nicely in *Consumer Culture and Postmodernism*, "The popular tradition of carnivals, fairs, and festivals provided symbolic inversions and transgressions of the official 'civilized' culture and favored excitement, uncontrolled emotions, and the direct and vulgar grotesque bodily pleasures of fattening food, intoxicating drink, and sexual promiscuity. These were *liminal* spaces in which the everyday world was turned upside down and in which the tattooed and the fantastic were possible, in which fantastic dreams could be expressed."[26] Just as vulgar modern fascinations would later play out in the bowels of the modern city, ancient fairs offered experiences well outside of the official civilizing processes of their time. More than just sites established for the exchange of commodities, fairs offered "spectacular imagery, bizarre juxtapositions, confusions of boundaries, and an immersion in a *mêlée* of strange sounds, motions, images, people, animals, and things."[27] Often seemingly unconnected to the real world, these ancient fairs and markets were sites of "the transformation of popular tradition through the intersection of different cultures." Bringing together "the exotic and the familiar, the villager and the townsman," they presented exotic and strange commodities from different parts of the world while strange signs, costumes, and languages appeared in a flood of "freaks, spectacles, and performances that stimulated desire and excitement."[28] As the industrial age began, these fascinations would mutate and migrate to the city, the slum, the seaside resort, the music hall, and the early department store. Eventually such mutations would find a home in the urban marketplace where they would play their part in the spinning of the vast all-encompassing web that today constitutes our current consumer culture. At the same time, a modern fascination fabricated from cultural memories of the crude pageantry of ancient fairs, festivals, and carnivals would begin to emerge as a central theme in modern art, literature, and theater.

The Development of Consumer Culture

It is a long way from the drab utilitarian products that filled the crude stalls of the medieval fair to the neon galaxies of luxury goods that populate the modern marketplace. Likewise, it is a long way from the simple peasants who traded at those ancient fairs to the stylish consumers of today who continually re-invent themselves in orgies of unbridled consumption. How did we get from Bartholemew Fair to Bloomingdale's? What happened?

---

[26] Featherstone, *Consumer Culture and Postmodernism*, 22.
[27] Featherstone, *Consumer Culture and Postmodernism*, 23.
[28] Featherstone, *Consumer Culture and Postmodernism*, 79.

There are those who would simply say that the Industrial Revolution happened, but this is far too easy. Following Marx, this attempts to explain the complex world of modern consumption as a derivative of modern production. Such one-dimensional explanations spark objections from those who insist that changes in consumer dynamics also originated in the social or the cultural sphere and became catalysts in the development of modern capitalism. These debates take many forms. One theory holds that changes in consumption originated with the rise of the bourgeoisie and that class's aspirations for upward social mobility. In this view, increased demand for luxury goods was fueled by the new merchant class's drive to emulate aristocratic patterns of consumption. As the prevailing class structure became more and more fluid, many scholars insisted that this kind of "conspicuous consumption," as Thorstein Veblen labeled it,[29] characterized a highly dynamic and richly symbolic commodity world independent of the circumstances of production. At the very least, the conventional wisdom insisted that changes in consumption beget changes in production as well as the other way around. This school of thought holds that the consumer revolution was "the necessary analogue to the industrial revolution, the necessary convulsion on the demand side of the equation to match convulsion of the supply side."[30] Others like Max Weber argued that early consumerism arose as part of the Enlightenment in an atmosphere of expanding "rationalism," which stressed worldly goals. [31] Weber insisted that Protestantism, with its individualistic, calculative form of salvation, stressing disciplined work and worldly accumulation, "sanctified character traits required by modern capitalism."[32] Following Weber, many have speculated that modern Romanticism, and not modern Protestantism, lay at the root of the consumer revolution. Romanticism, they say, brought with it a certain type of materialistic "hedonism" entailing a lust for new experiences; for self-improvement, aesthetic enjoyment, and novelty; and for the dream-like illusions found in the commodity. As one scholar puts it, the Romantic continually "withdraws from reality as fast as he encounters it, evercasting [sic] his daydreams forward in time, attaching them to the

---

[29] Thorstein Veblen, *The Theory of the Leisure Class*, 1899, (London: MacMillan, 1994).

[30] Neil McKendrick, "Commercialization and the Economy," in Neil McKendrick, et al. ed., *The Birth of Consumer Society: The Commercialization of Eighteenth-Century England* (Bloomington: Indiana University Press, 1982), 9, quoted in Sassatelli, *Consumer Culture*, 15.

[31] Max Weber, *The Protestant Ethic and the Spirit of Capitalism*, 1904 (London: Allen and Unwin, 1930).

[32] Lawrence Cahoone, "Max Weber," in Lawrence Cahoone, ed., *From Modernism to Postmodernism: An Anthology*. Second Edition (Malden, MA: Blackwell Publishing, 2003), 127.

objects of desire...."[33] This kind of modern hedonism is not a hedonism of the body, but rather of the mind, and consequently it is infinite. Put another way, "the body and its desires, are no longer sated by the banquets of old: the mind and the myriad meanings it can give to the experience of things extend the possibilities of consumption to infinity."[34] Finally, still others have attributed the beginnings of the consumer revolution to the emergence of modern markets and marketing.

Today, most scholars agree that modern patterns of consumption began to develop before the capitalist era, or at least contemporaneously with it, and certainly well before the industrial revolution. Further, most believe that this so-called consumer revolution exhibited substantial social and cultural components, and that these components led mysterious lives lived well beyond the influence of the organization of modern production. The appearance of modern modes of consumption whether Protestant, Romantic, or hedonistic in origin—whether driven by class consciousness or market development—involved a slow social and economic evolution of increasingly materialistic mentalities, powerful impulses toward accumulation, and marked affinities for novelty and luxury goods. Sparked by international commerce, colonization, courtly excess, and a speeding up of the dynamics of fashion and taste brought on by increased social mobility and changes in techniques of advertising and promotion,[35] the modern consumer emerged not only from the flash of industrial and technological progress but also from the slow cauldron of social and cultural evolution.

The ongoing "chicken or egg" debates over whether these early upheavals in consumer behavior were the result of emerging capitalism or resulted in capitalism's emergence are perhaps best resolved by saying that they were both causes *and* effects of the great economic upheavals that followed the Renaissance and the Enlightenment. Although it may be true that modern patterns of consumption had origins outside of capitalism, it must be remembered that capitalism generally has, as perhaps its most notable feature, the tendency and power to perpetuate conditions that are hospitable to its well-being and growth. Any form of consumer behavior that serves to perpetuate the system is immediately embraced, nurtured, expanded, and reproduced, thus giving the appearance of being an organic result of its capitalistic underpinnings.

In one way or another, all these theories fit the historical mold. One can see evidence of the beginnings of today's consumer culture in the

---

[33] Colin Campbell, *The Romantic Ethic and the Spirit of Modern Consumerism* (Oxford: Basil Blackwell, 1987), 86-7, quoted in Sassatelli, *Consumer Culture*, 17.

[34] Sassatelli, *Consumer Culture*, 17.

[35] Sassatelli, *Consumer Culture*, 10.

Renaissance marketplace where the appearance of new needs and new means of attributing value to commodities were linked to the appearance of new types of commodities especially to non-essential goods from the far corners of a widening world: luxuries like spices, perfumes, dyes, silk, linen, sugar, coffee, tea, and cocoa. New economies based on trade begot new societies, especially in Italy, England, Germany, and Holland, where the consumption of luxury goods contributed to the accumulation of capital, thus satisfying one of the prerequisites for the development of modern industry. All this sparked marked societal and cultural changes hospitable to new lifestyles that were characterized by self-indulgence and hedonism, lifestyles that by the middle of the seventeenth century had begun to embrace a new recreational attitude toward purchasing. In this change, we can see the first crude operations of modern consumer culture. Cities arose, supported by a robust merchant middle class staffing permanent urban marketplaces that replaced the transitory fairs of old. In these great trading centers, Europe witnessed the democratization of luxury and style accompanied by a startling increase in the velocity of fashion. Shops were no longer solely the places of trade, but quickly became places of entertainment, refinement, amusement, and leisure. During the eighteenth and nineteenth centuries in Europe, the emerging popular culture began to weave its gossamer web, creating new societies and cultures of consumption and transforming the spaces where consumption occurred into exotic dream worlds. Shop owners became masters of display. Artificial lighting and large glass windows appeared as merchants labored to create spectacles that would not only expose the allure and the accessibility of their wares but also mediate their meaning. It was not a long jump from this to the department store, the World's Fair, and the Paris Arcades.

Some Early Examples of Consumer Culture

As the nineteenth century unfolded, examples of the growing influence of an adolescent consumer culture began to appear in the grand capitals of Europe—in London, Paris and Berlin—first in the shopping districts and in fine shops, and later in grand glassed-in arcades and in the new department stores that became the rage after 1850. By late century, these cities and many others had, themselves, become part of the growing spectacle. Everywhere there appeared dream landscapes and artificial realities of commodity display and architectural fantasy spawned by the new industrial process of mass production and the creation of leisure time for the masses.

Early department stores offer perhaps the first clear example of this new culture's power to attract, mesmerize, displace, and distract enormous crowds of browsers and customers. Employing fantastic displays that flaunted wide assortments of luxury products, these artificial dream worlds no longer presented shopping as a rational, utilitarian, economic necessity, but rather as a leisure-time cultural activity. By 1850, Bon Marche in Paris and Harrod's in London had organized and orchestrated the shopping experience into a dreamscape. These new palaces of the commodity provoked exotic dreams and offered eclectic experiences and illusions designed not only to sell products but also to blur the distinction between commerce and culture. They were soon joined by Kaufhaus in Berlin, Macy's in New York, Marshall Fields in Chicago, and by similar institutions around the world. Even though a fully developed consumer culture would not begin to enfold the whole of American society in its all-embracing grasp until the last decades of the twentieth century, the early department stores of Europe and America clearly illustrate that many of the techniques that this culture still employs were perfected over a hundred years before the period of its total cultural dominance.

Even more illustrative of the intoxicating power of the emerging modern consumer culture were the great Trade Fairs and Expositions of the nineteenth century. Resembling nothing so much as early manifestations of today's theme parks, the Great Expositions held between 1850 and the first decades of the twentieth century not only constituted fantastic commercial displays of the commodities and luxuries of their age, but they also manipulated these spectacles by hitching them to emotionally powerful engines of national pride. In addition, they appealed to a growing faith in the progress of modernity. Here in the great trade fairs of Europe and America, we find an early voice of one of the modern consumer culture's most enduring themes: that mass production is a bridge to one's personal dreams—that industrial progress and the products it creates lead to individual fulfillment. In the great Trade Expositions and World's Fairs of the nineteenth century, "reality becomes artificial, a phantasmagoria of commodities and architectural constructs made possible by the new industrial process."[36]

The first of these great exhibitions was held in London's Hyde Park in 1851. Officially christened "The Great Exhibition of the Works of Industry of all Nations," the fair featured over 13,000 exhibits showcased in Sir Joseph Paxton's enormous Crystal Palace, a fantasy construction of iron and glass enclosing almost a million square feet. Conceived by Prince

[36] Susan Buck-Moss "Benjamin's *Passagen-Werk*," *New German Critique*, 1983, 29, quoted in Featherstone, *Consumer Culture and Postmodernism*, 73.

Albert and intended to flaunt the blossoming industrial might that was propelling Great Britain toward unrivaled world power, the 1851 London Exhibition featured a vast assortment of tools, appliances, machinery, and other commodities from around the world presented in spectacular displays that intensified the market experience into "a managed dreamscape."[37] Throughout the remainder of the nineteenth century and the first half of the twentieth century, hundreds of these trade fairs and exhibitions were held around the world. In 1888 alone, for example, fairs were held in Melbourne, Glasgow, Brussels, Barcelona, Copenhagen, and Lisbon. All manifested the early workings of modern consumer culture.

Perhaps the best example is the World's Columbian Exposition held in Chicago in 1893. Here America began to rightly assert her growing preeminence in industrialization, manufacturing, and business, while at the same time, perhaps less rightly, she sought to demonstrate her cultural parity with Europe. Part midway, part cultural exhibit, part commercial merchandise mart, the great fair at Chicago attracted millions of visitors from all over the world and sparked intense debate in America. Through all the vulgar attractions wrapped in cultural pretense, the message of consumption showed clearly in an odd mixing of art and commerce. It can be no coincidence that the largest and most magnificent building at the Chicago fair was the Manufactures and Liberal Arts building. Driving home one of popular culture's favorite themes, the mixing of manufacturing and the arts, lending cultural validation to manufacturing, while at the same time presenting art as something that could be mass produced, commodified, and sold.

In the 1893 Columbian Exposition, the voice of the newly emerging American consumer culture could be clearly heard amidst exuberant nationalist expressions and joyous celebrations of American nationalism, industrialization, technological leadership and financial might. As historian Phil Patton puts it, the Fair was "a dry run for the mass marketing, packing and advertising" that would follow in the twentieth century.[38] Perhaps most importantly, the Fair had a lasting impact, valorizing consumption on many levels and indelibly branding on the national consciousness the notion that personal enjoyment is directly tied to purchasing goods and spending money.

Reading the contemporary reactions to the Chicago Fair is like reading prophetic visions. Harvard president, Charles Eliot Nelson, himself one of the directors of the Columbian Exposition, wrote of the exposition's

[37] Don Slater, "Going Shopping: Markets, Crowds, and Consumption," in Chris Jenks, ed., *Cultural Reproduction* (London and New York: Routledge, 1993).
[38] Phil Patton, "Sell the Cookstove if Necessary, but Come to the Fair," in *Smithsonian* (June, 1993) 24: 38-50.

"incongruities, its mingling of noble realities and ignoble pretenses,...its refinement cheek-by-jowl with vulgarities,...its order and confusion...."[39] While, more to the point, Henry Adams wrote, "I am puzzled to understand the final impression left on the average mind...as to the inward meaning of this dream of beauty. Of course, I don't understand it, but then I don't understand anything...."[40] Clearly, these critics sensed the presence of the beginnings of a new cultural force at Chicago. Clearly, they felt the attraction of an invisible power reinforcing its mantra by associating progress with commerce and by injecting joy, mystery, and excitement into the simple act of consumption.

European observers of the great continental fairs of the nineteenth century sensed a similar presence. Writing in the 1930s, Walter Benjamin, a devoted student of the age of the great fairs in Paris, declared the early World Exhibitions held in that city in 1855, 1867, 1878, 1889, and 1900 to be "places of pilgrimage to the commodity fetish." There can be little doubt that Benjamin clearly saw the footprint of an emerging new culture in the great Paris Exhibition of 1867. His prose relating to the event is filled with compelling allusions: calling the exhibits "phantasmagoria which a person enters in order to be distracted," finding everywhere "the enthronement of the commodity with its luster of distraction," and declaring the fair to be the point at which "capitalist culture attains its most radiant unfolding." In his study of the mid-nineteenth-century French romantic poet, Charles Baudelaire, Benjamin declares that the Great Paris Exhibition of 1867 "propagate(d) the universe of the commodity," and in its shadow, he pronounces the Second Empire to be "at the height of its power" and Paris to be the "capital of luxury and fashion."[41]

Walter Benjamin and Charles Baudelaire

Among the very first to sense the presence and the character of this new cultural force and to attempt to intellectually penetrate its complex workings was the German intellectual, writer, critic, and translator, Walter Benjamin, whose pioneering ideas regarding history, literature, language, and emerging consumer culture were to prove astoundingly prophetic. Writing primarily in the 1930s, Benjamin was so far ahead of his time that at first only a handful of European intellectuals had any idea what he was talking about. It was not until the complex notions that would come to characterize postmodern thought began to emerge in the late 1960s that

---

[39] Patton, "Sell the Cookstove if Necessary," 24: 38-50.

[40] Henry Adams in a letter to Lucy Baxter, October 18, 1893.

[41] Walter Benjamin, "Paris Capital of the Nineteenth Century," in *The Writer of Modern Life*, 36-7.

Walter Benjamin's abstract and seemingly disjointed "ramblings" began to make sense to a wider audience.

Two ghosts stalk almost all Walter Benjamin's work: the sad, haunting apparition of Charles Baudelaire and the stern, analytical specter of Karl Marx. In the poems of the great, mid-nineteenth-century, romantic poet, Charles Baudelaire, Benjamin found vibrant Marxian allegories that, for him, "made present" the character of the Baudelairian age and lay open the evolving structures and mechanisms of emerging modernity. Everywhere in Baudelaire, Walter Benjamin found allusions to a blossoming consumer culture with its early dream-like displays of the modern commodity and its blinding ability to suppress human reason, to fascinate, and to seduce.

In his essays on Baudelaire's Paris, the best of which were intended to be part of a longer work entitled, *Charles Baudelaire, A Lyric Poet in the Era of High Capitalism*, Benjamin makes constant reference to the ideas of Marx. These essays abound with references to mid-nineteenth century "pilgrimages to commodity fetishism," "glorification of the exchange value of the commodity," and "propagation of the universe of the commodity." In "Paris, the Capital of the Nineteenth Century," Benjamin informs us that, "Fashion prescribes the ritual according to which the commodity fetish demands to be worshipped."[42]

In another example, Benjamin focuses on "Le Voyage," the last poem in Baudelaire's great cycle, *Les Fleurs du Mal* (The Flowers of Evil). For Benjamin, Baudelaire's concluding lines conjure images of the "phantasmagoria," an eighteenth-century optical device used to project shadows of moving figures onto walls or screens. Throughout his work, Walter Benjamin uses the metaphor of these eerie shadow-producing contrivances to stand for Marxian notions of commodity fetishism, for false consciousness, and for the powerful cultural forces that mask the realities of modern life. In "Le Voyage," the poet alludes to travel "Deep in the unknown to find the new,"[43] and in response Benjamin writes:

> Newness is a quality independent of the use value of the commodity. It is the origin of the semblance that belongs inalienably to images produced by the collective unconscious. It is the quintes-sence of that false consciousness whose indefatigable agent is fashion. This semblance of the new is reflected, like one mirror in another, in the semblance of the ever recurrent. The product of this reflection

---

[42] Walter Benjamin, "Paris Capital of the Nineteenth Century," in *The Writer of Modern Life*, 36-7.

[43] Charles Baudelaire, "The Voyage," in *Les Fleurs du Mal*, trans. Richard Howard (Boston: David R. Godine, 1982), 156-7.

is the phantasmagoria of 'cultural history' in which the bourgeoisie enjoys its false consciousness to the full.[44]

One might conclude that such leaps are the result of reading too much into the text. Is this not a clear case of Walter Benjamin finding in Baudelaire's seemingly straightforward verse complex Marxian allusions to the evils of emerging commodity capitalism when the great poet intended no such imagery? Is this not an attempt to forcibly pry from Baudelaire's dark, vaguely romantic verses of sex and death images of fantastic display and consumption, blinding allusions to numbing commercialization, allegories for alienation and "the gradual denaturing of art as it is submersed in commodification and fashion?"[45] Indeed, Benjamin's reading of Baudelaire seems so extreme that it is difficult to conclude otherwise. However, to so conclude would constitute a misreading, not necessarily of Charles Baudelaire but of Walter Benjamin.

Among Benjamin's most revolutionary concepts was the idea that works of art could be read, not for their reflection of the past, but rather for what the present could bring to bear upon them. His 1931 essay "Literary History and the Study of Literature" makes his idea clear. "What is at stake is not to portray literary works in the context of their age, but to represent the age that perceives them—our age—in the age during which they arose." This, Benjamin insisted, makes literature, not the lifeless and distorted "material of history," but rather a living "organ of history."[46]

In the 1930s Walter Benjamin had surely glimpsed a clear picture of an emerging consumer culture and guessed at its power to dominate the future. It is equally clear that he saw in the poems of Charles Baudelaire the beginnings of this culture in mid-nineteenth century Parisian street life. Whether or not Charles Baudelaire intended any of this is quite another matter. Although his poetry contains little direct reference to the spectacle of the commodity and no specific Marxist imagery, we know that Baudelaire, like Benjamin after him, was deeply wounded by notions concerning the hollowness and isolation of modern life. Late in 1863, Baudelaire published an essay called "The Painter of Modern Life," in which he foreshadowed many of the later themes of Walter Benjamin: "the increasing importance of fashion; the replacement of permanence and solidity with transience and fragmentation;...the descent of (artistic) genius into 'convalescence'; the importance of such marginal figures as the 'dandy' and the 'flâneur'; the

---

[44] Walter Benjamin, "Paris Capital of the Nineteenth Century," in *The Writer of Modern Life*, 41-2.

[45] Jennings, Introduction to Walter Benjamin, in *The Writer of Modern Life*, 9.

[46] Walter Benjamin, "Literary History and the Study of Literature," in *Selected Writings*, ed. Marcus Bullock and Michael W. Jennings, trans. Harry Zohn (Cambridge MA: Harvard University Press, 1999), 2:464.

isolation and alienation of the modern individual in the urban crowd;...and even the sounding of the theme of phantasmagoria."[47]

Certainly, Baudelaire was a revolutionary of sorts, but unlike Benjamin, he could not have been much of a theoretical Marxist, having published *Les Fleurs du Mal* ten years before Marx published *Das Kapital*. His politics were not those of the intellectual, but rather those of the bourgeois outcast, the downtrodden artist, the angry conspirator eager to accomplish the overthrow of the present regime but ungrounded and with no thought to the system that would follow. As Benjamin later wrote in his notes to "The Paris of the Second Empire in Baudelaire," "Baudelaire was a secret agent— an agent of the secret discontent of his class with its own rule."[48] Baudelaire knew nothing of commodity fetishism, and to be sure he intended none of the rich Marxian theoretical imagery that Walter Benjamin found oozing from almost every line.

In Benjamin's view, Charles Baudelaire was not a great all-seeing poetic genius who gathered and distilled the essence of his age. As Benjamin saw it, the poet was not the master of his own age but rather a sensitive outcast totally battered by it. In his view, Baudelaire did not rise above his age: he surrendered himself to its modern ruptures, brokenness, falsehoods, and shocks. As Michael Jennings puts it, "For Benjamin, the greatness of Baudelaire consists...in his absolute *susceptibility* to the worst excesses of modern life: Baudelaire was in possession, not of genius, but of an extraordinary 'sensitive disposition' that enabled him to perceive, through a painful empathy, the character of the age."[49] That character is revealed in devastatingly beautiful verse filled with ambiguity and alienation, not with Marxist imagery nor with allusions to the world of the commodity, but with images of woman, of death, and perhaps most tellingly, of Paris. It was Walter Benjamin, not Charles Baudelaire, who defined the character of mid-nineteenth century Paris as one of thoroughgoing commodification accomplishing "the poetization of the banal." True to his own visions of the critic's responsibility, Walter Benjamin was "representing his own age" and his own convictions in his radical readings of Baudelaire's dark ponderings of the previous era.

---

[47] Jennings, Introduction to Walter Benjamin, in *The Writer of Modern Life*, 24; Charles Baudelaire, "The Painter of Modern Life," in *The Painter of Modern Life and Other Essays* (Oxford: Phaidon Press, 1964).

[48] Walter Benjamin, Addendum to "The Paris of the Second Empire in Baudelaire," in *Charles Baudelaire: A Lyric Poet in the Era of High Capitalism*, trans. Harry Zohn (London: Verso, 1983), 104.

[49] Jennings, "Introduction to Walter Benjamin" in *The Writer of Modern Life*, 15.

Many of Walter Benjamin's short pieces on Charles Baudelaire were intended to be parts of the central section of his masterwork, *Die Passagewerken* (*The Arcades Project*). Begun in the late 1920s, the massive work was to be a detailed study of mid-nineteenth-century Paris and the infancy of consumer culture. It was never completed, and after Benjamin's apparent suicide in 1940, the completed portions of the manuscript were thought lost. Then in 1979 portions of the work along with Benjamin's notes turned up among the papers of one of Benjamin's associates in the *Bibliothèque Nationale* in Paris. Thus it was not until the early 1980s, over forty years after Walter Benjamin's death, that his masterpiece saw publication in the original German. The complete English language edition did not appear until 1999. These pages contained Walter Benjamin's vision of the beginnings of the reign of the commodity, and Charles Baudelaire stands as the central figure in this remarkably detailed study.

The Arcades Project took its title from the vast complex of urban mercantile galleries and arcades that had begun to cover Paris by the middle of the nineteenth century. With their shinning iron and glass construction, labyrinthine passageways, and fantastic displays of luxury goods, the Paris Arcades were a "world in miniature," the forerunners of the modern department store, and these gleaming palaces supplied Walter Benjamin with the perfect organizing metaphor for his investigations into the emergence of consumer culture. Interiors without exterior, both interior and exterior at the same time, at once street and market and amusement palace, these shop-lined fantasy worlds of consumption reflected the ambiguity that both Benjamin and Baudelaire saw in the bourgeois experience of the era. As Benjamin, himself, put it, the experiences of life determined by commodity production, "present themselves as phantasmagoria."[50] There can be little doubt that when he spoke of phantasmagoria, Walter Benjamin was talking about his clear vision of the powerful new cultural force.

Both Baudelaire and Benjamin were insightful pioneers exploring the emerging mysteries of a new culture of the consumer even though they interpreted what they saw in very different ways. Despite these differences, Walter Benjamin developed a deep sense of identification with the life and work of Charles Baudelaire. Both men were outcasts of a sort, artists whose work was largely ignored by their contemporaries; both were stripped of the possession and security of bourgeois life; both took refuge in the street, in the crowd, in drugs; and perhaps most importantly, both men saw themselves

---

[50] Walter Benjamin, *Gesammelte Schriften*, ed. Rolf Tiedemann and Herman Schweppenäuser (Frankfurt: Suhrkamp Verlag, 1972), 5:1256-8, quoted in Jennings, "Introduction to Walter Benjamin" in *The Writer of Modern Life*, 9.

the *flâneur*, a familiar character in Baudelaire's Paris and a character in whom Walter Benjamin found a protagonist of sorts for life work, *The Arcades Project*.

For Benjamin, following Baudelaire, the *flâneur* was the anonymous "stroller" wandering the dream-like urban spaces of the great city. Lost in the crowd, he meanders, buffeted by modernity's artificiality, randomness, and shock, and by the fantastic fictions and strange values of the fashions and displays of modern city life. The character of Baudelaire's urban wanderer is perfect for Benjamin's purposes. "The intoxication to which the *flâneur* surrenders," Benjamin informs us in "Paris of the Second Empire in Baudelaire," "is the intoxication of the commodity immersed in a surging stream of customers."[51] In "Paris, Capital of the Nineteenth Century," Benjamin comes to the heart of the matter.

> The department store (Arcades) is the last promenade of the *flâneur*. In the *flâneur*, the intelligentsia sets foot in the marketplace— ostensibly to look around, but in truth to find a buyer."[52]

Here we find the central point of identification, the common bond between Walter Benjamin and Charles Baudelaire. Both men sensed a cultural shift, and both saw the future of the commodity as a future in which everything would be commodified: information, knowledge, literature, art, even culture itself. Walter Benjamin sees both himself and Baudelaire in Baudelaire's image of the artist as *flâneur*: both buyer and seller, both the impassive observer of and the willing accomplice to the deceptive fascinations of an emerging consumer culture with its "phantasmagoria" of gleaming commodity display and spectacle. Although they came at it from very difference angles, both men reached similar conclusions. To use Walter Benjamin's compelling words, both men recognized "the monuments of the bourgeoisie as ruins even before they...crumbled."[53]

Max Horkheimer and Theodor Adorno

In the 1930s, Walter Benjamin was not the only one contemplating the teetering "monuments of the bourgeoisie." Benjamin had close ties to Max Horkheimer and Theodor Adorno, the founders of the so-called Frankfurt School of social theory. Responding to a perceived oppressive rationality embedded in modern society, the Frankfurt School sought to develop a

---

[51] Walter Benjamin, "Paris of the Second Empire in Baudelaire," in *The Writer of Modern Life*, 85.

[52] Walter Benjamin, "Paris Capital of the Nineteenth Century," in *The Writer of Modern Life*, 40.

[53] Walter Benjamin, "Paris, Capital of the Nineteenth Century," in *The Writer of Modern Life*, 45.

comprehensive, self-reflective body of theory aimed at exposing what they saw as the growing domination, alienation, and "barbarism" of advanced Western industrial civilization. The resulting body of work, collectively known as Critical Theory, turned on the idea that both modern capitalism and modern communism had either suppressed or absorbed all the voices of positive change, thus creating self-perpetuating cultures of domination. As part of their monumental quest, Horkheimer and Adorno set out to identify those dark consequences of modernity that Marx had failed to foresee. Among these were the unexpectedly persuasive powers of a rapidly maturing consumer culture, that seductive, pacifying dream world of the consumer marketplace. As the critical theorists saw it, a large part of this growing culture's growing power was sustained by marketing and the unbreakable links that mass-media and advertising create between production and consumption, links that are forged in the furnaces of what they call "the culture industry." In their well-known essay, "The Culture Industry: Enlightenment as Mass Deception," which, not coincidentally, was written during their exile in the United States, and appeared in their 1944 work, *The Dialects of Enlightenment*, Horkheimer and Adorno describe the culture industry as a highly specialized industrial sector producing diffuse images and elaborating complex symbols aimed at the manipulation and conformity of Western society. Although Horkheimer and Adorno, saw the culture industry as primarily an enslaving arm of capitalist production and were reticent to acknowledge that the relationship between production and consumption was a complex two-way street, their early examinations of popular culture and the media were the first to suggest the kind of domination that the emerging popular culture would soon imposes.

"The Culture Industry" is a document of chilling content. In this Orwellian chronicle of commodification, mass media, and mass deception, Horkheimer and Adorno pull no punches. Explaining how the market's conventional wisdom seeks to justify the manipulative media productions of the culture industry, they point to the familiar rationale of technology, which they warn is the rationale "of domination itself," a "circle of manipulation and retroactive need in which the utility of the system grows stronger." [54] Furthermore, Horkheimer and Adorno insist that the public is not only the victim of such manipulations, but is duped into becoming a willing participant in the process. With the public on board, "the people on top are no longer interested in concealing the monopoly; as its violence becomes

---

[54] Theodor W. Adorno and Max Horkheimer, "The Culture Industry: Enlightenment as Mass Deception," in *The Dialectics of Enlightenment*, 1944, in Schor and Holt, *Consumer Society Reader*, 4.

more open, so its power grows." "The Culture Industry" is an ironic story of indoctrination and mass deception, detailing "the triumph of invested capital, whose title as absolute master," Horkheimer and Adorno insist, "is etched into our hearts," an irresistible ideology that is firmly believed even by "the dispossessed in the employment line."[55]

This kind of blinding ideology, Critical Theory tells us, is a tale that is "the mingled content of every film, whatever the plot...."[56] With such chilling revelations, the culture industry opens its homogenizing arms to all:

> Something is provided for all so that none may escape; the distinc-
> tions are emphasized and extended. The public is catered to with a
> hierarchal range of mass-produced products of varying quality, thus
> advancing the rule of complete quantification. Everybody must behave
> (as if spontaneously) in accordance with his previously determined
> and indexed level and choose the category of mass product turned out
> for his type. Consumers appear as statistics on research organization
> charts, and are divided by income groups into red, green, and blue
> areas; the technique is that used for any type of propaganda.[57]

In the end, Horkheimer and Adorno conclude that the new culture accomplishes the regimented fusion of culture and entertainment, a fusion that melds all the arts into one work,[58] a single all-encompassing debased work that ties us to the illusions of the commodity and stamps us all with the mold of uniformity. "From every sound film and every broadcast program the social effect can be inferred which is exclusive to none and shared by all. The culture industry has molded men as a type unfailingly reproduced in every product."[59] By disseminating a "naked lie" that what exists should exist, cultural commodities turn facts into values. According to Adorno, late capitalism is sustained by the tireless intellectual reduplication of everything that is. The message of the culture industry is that things should not, and indeed cannot, be changed and that existing forms of consciousness and the intellectual status quo are not only appropriate but also unassailable owing simply to the fact of their own existence.[60]

In the end, Horkheimer and Adorno conclude that the culture industry successfully presents us with amusements to create the illusion that "the outside world is the straightforward continuation of that presented on the

[55] Adorno and Horkheimer, "The Culture Industry," 6.
[56] Adorno and Horkheimer, "The Culture Industry," 6.
[57] Adorno and Horkheimer, "The Culture Industry," 5.
[58] Adorno and Horkheimer, "The Culture Industry," 6.
[59] Adorno and Horkheimer, "The Culture Industry," 7.
[60] Deborah Cook, *The Culture Industry Revisited: Theodor W. Adorno on Mass Culture*, Landham
MD: Rowand and Littlefield, 1996, 86-7.

screen."[61] We are thus rendered helpless, not by our flight from reality, but by having been freed from "the last remaining thought of resistance."[62] These lines, written in 1944, would prove prophetic years before television was perfected and marketed. The rising power of mass media to pacify viewers and to manipulate the needs of the consumer was clear to these visionaries of Critical Theory. They understood that the culture industry was well on its way to becoming the workshop of consumer culture.

John Kenneth Galbraith and Daniel Bell

By the middle of the twentieth century, it was becoming clear to almost everyone that the early critics of the industrial age had been right, that modern progress came at a numbing price. In this period, consumer culture was beginning to consolidate its awesome power in the United States, the American electronic media were beginning to flex new technological muscles, and a pervasive, new, distinctly American, popular culture was emerging. Nonetheless, mid-century observers of the modern condition largely overlooked these cultural phenomena, remaining generally focused on social issues and on the conventional woes of so-called mass-society, woes like conformity, loss of identity, and growing notions of powerlessness and alienation. However, as the consumer revolution exploded into the post-World War II era, its far-reaching effects were impossible to ignore, and most critics of the era were compelled to at least comment.

One of the most visible of these pundits was John Kenneth Galbraith, whose widely read study *The Affluent Society* was published in 1958. Following Horkheimer and Adorno and the rest of the Frankfurt School, Galbraith stressed the role of marketing and advertising in precipitating a shift from a consumer-driven marketplace to a marketplace in which large businesses and manufacturers controlled market rhythm and content. At the bottom of this shift, according to Galbraith, lay the increasing affluence of American consumers, who laid themselves open to manipulation because they had become "so far removed from physical want that they do not...know what they want."[63]

Whereas John Galbraith's vision of the emergence of consumer culture corresponded to the Marxian view in which the mode of production controls all social and cultural spheres including consumption, there were others in this period who insisted that the mode of production, although historically instrumental in shaping our society and our culture, does not universally

---

[61] Adorno and Horkheimer, "The Culture Industry," 7.
[62] Adorno and Horkheimer, "The Culture Industry," 15.
[63] John Kenneth Galbraith, *The Affluent Society* (London: Andre Deutsch, 1958), 131.

control and unify society. Perhaps the best-known of these critics is Daniel Bell, whose 1973 study, *The Coming of Post-Industrial Society*, championed much more complex theories of society and the marketplace. For Bell, the post-industrial marketplace was characterized by the exchange of knowledge as the seminal commodity:

> Broadly speaking, if industrial society is based on machine tech-
> nology, post-industrial society is shaped by an intelligent technology.
> And if capital and labor are the major structural features of industrial
> society, information and knowledge are those of the post-industrial
> society.[64]

This gave a new spin to commodities and implied a much more complex marketplace. Knowledge is not a material economic product; it is a social product, and the notion of its commodification presupposed the computerized technologies of the information age, predicted the change from a manufacturing to a service economy, and suggested a future need for cooperative strategies to combat what Bell saw as a series of emerging "unhealthy and profoundly pathological cultural contradictions."[65] Nonetheless, Bell insisted that the post-industrial world was not replacing the conventional industrial world, and he offered only limited insight as to how new "intelligent technologies" might influence the conventional marketplace. Still, Bell's insights into the commodification of knowledge pointed directly to the development of the communications, information, and entertainment technologies that were soon to become indispensable tools employed by the new consumer culture to accomplish its most spectacular slight-of-hand: the commodification of art and finally and most disturbingly of culture itself.

Modernism and Postmodernism

At the time they wrote, it is unlikely that any of these great critics of the Modern Age envisioned the remarkable conclusion toward which many of their ideas were pointing. Although they sensed its presence, neither Horkheimer nor Adorno nor Galbraith nor Bell nor even the transcendent, intellectual mystic, Walter Benjamin, could have imagined the extent of a blossoming consumer culture's future power. No one could have imagined that, employing the endless reproduction and far-reaching dissemination made possible by the new technology, this blossoming cultural force would suck into its glowing translucent aura all of fine art and high culture—all of

---

[64] Daniel Bell, "Forward, 1976," in *The Coming of Post-Industrial Society* (New York: Basic Books, 1976), ix-xxii, in Cahoone, *From Modernism to Postmodernism*, 209-17
[65] Sassatelli, *Consumer Culture*, 118.

the avant-garde, all of the voices of enlightenment, all criticism, literature, music, beauty, protest—suck it all in and swirl it around in the Day-Glo cauldrons of a base and depthless popular culture to create endlessly varied lines of mass-produced new cultural products. None could have guessed that by the late 1970s there would be those bold enough to suggest that the new culture of late-Capitalism was transcendent and that the Age of Science and Reason had come to an end.

Whether we choose to call such speculations late modern or postmodern, our consumer culture remains the same, just as the aim of this book remains an immediate and accessible description of this powerfully active cultural phenomena. This book's goal is not only to discuss theory and conceptual matters, but also to illustrate these ideas with copious, simple, tangible, straightforward examples of consumer culture at work as it appears in all its many forms in everyday life. Accordingly, this book does not take a wholly postmodernism approach because discussions of the postmodern quite necessarily *cannot* be simple, tangible, or straightforward. Despite its extraordinary and insightful conceptual usefulness, postmodernism is by its very nature complex, paradoxical, contingent, impossibly interconnected, and convoluted; and thus, a simple, "straightforward discussion" of anything postmodern constitutes an oxymoron. What is more, today a growing number of scholars are beginning to suspect that Postmodernism is dead. Whatever the case, it remains the subject of an enormous amount of confounding controversy, and this book would be woefully incomplete without giving the postmodern its due, for postmodern thinkers have contributed enormously to our understanding of the ubiquitous cultural phenomenon we seek to explore.

Following the subtitle of Fredric Jameson's famous book, we might begin by saying that today's consumer culture is part of *The Cultural Logic of Late Capitalism*.[66] Undoubtedly this is true, but sadly it takes Jameson over 400 often numbing pages to explain what he means by this. Nonetheless, this is a good place to begin, for "the cultural logic of late capitalism," is, in large part, our theme, and in many ways, it does not matter whether one chooses to call it modern or postmodern. After all, the modern is contained within the postmodern and vice versa, and the difference is often simply a question of semantics or of one's personal convictions and point of view.

Certainly, it can be safely said that, at least up to a point and beginning at its most fundamental level, the Modern's critique of itself, and the Postmodern's critique of Modernity, are in many ways the same. Both hold that, despite the notable contributions of science and enlightened

---

[66] Jameson, *Postmodernism*.

reason to mankind's material well-being, the modern technological era has produced some unlovely side effects, namely alienation, loss of identity, homogenization, numbing bureaucracy, a chilling sense of powerlessness, runaway nationalism, and a pervasive false consciousness. The continued growth of exploitation, nationalism, war, sectarian violence, terrorism, poverty, environmental neglect, and man's uninterrupted inhumanity to man has led many to criticize the course of universal enlightenment and to question the benevolence of a world ruled by the systematic logic of science and instrumental reason. Indeed, such horrors have led many to suspect that all modern rational systems have the power to subvert, to reproduce themselves endlessly, and to serve their own purposes. At the same time, the world appears not to be struggling toward unity but accelerating toward fragmentation. In these notions, we find the seeds of postmodern thought.

All this notwithstanding, a detailed discussion of the origins and theories of postmodernism in these pages would constitute a monumental and parenthetic diversion. Accordingly, this book will focus only on postmodern thought as it relates to the present consumer culture and its manipulations. As for more general background, let us just say that the difference between a modern and a postmodern view of the current state of affairs is that the modernist still believes that rational systems can be effective, that the unified "project of enlightenment" can be salvaged, that the universal emancipation of mankind through science and reason is still possible, while the post modernist believes, or at least suspects, that the modern project has failed, that unity, truth, progress, universalism, hierarchal logic, and functional systemization have all flown apart into countless fragments, and that life now revolves around complexity, ambiguity, and a certain fluidity in the meaning of things.

What we have today come to call postmodernism has roots in all these critiques of the Modern Condition, and this new mode of thinking first came together in the work of a handful of radical French thinkers who surfaced in the 1970s: most notably Jean-François Lyotard and Jean Baudrillard.

Jean-François Lyotard and Jean Baudrillard

Among the most abstract of postmodernism's early intellectual champions was Jean-François Lyotard, whose vision of a "postmodern condition" sparked waves of new speculation hostile to unified, modern, intellectual constructs. Following Daniel Bell's notion of a post-industrial age in which knowledge was becoming the central principle of social organization, Lyotard postulated that knowledge was produced by dissent, "by putting into question existing paradigms, by inventing new ones, rather than by assenting to universal truth or agreeing to a consensus."[67] Like Bell, Lyotard saw the coming age as one of the primacy of computers, information, science, and technology and pointed to "the computerization of society."[68] Finding modern unified narratives and their notions of universality and certainty to be reductionist, simplistic, and oppressive, Lyotard championed modest, local, provisional discourses and introduced the micro-politics of the postmodern. Unlike many other early post modernist thinkers who tied the creation of images, spectacles, and simulations to desire and consumption, Lyotard tends to divorce such images from the process of social and cultural production, abstractly embracing them as "figural" stimulants of "singularity" that enhance "the intensity of life and the flow of desire."[69] Thus, for Lyotard, consumer culture may be more of a good thing than the evil deceiver described by so many of his critics, many of whom have pointed to his failure to recognize the way that capitalism exploits images and to a general lack of social theory and critique in his work. Indeed, most scholars would agree that Lyotard's work "carries a linguistic and philosophical turn which renders his theory more...abstract and distanced from the social realities and problems of the present age."[70] Nonetheless and although unlike his contemporary, Jean Baudrillard, he rarely addresses consumer culture head-on, Jean-François Lyotard's insights into the fluidities, uncertainties, and figural immersions of the so-called "postmodern condition," illuminate the state of mind that gave life to a mature consumer culture, a state of mind in which eclecticism is the "degree zero of contemporary general culture." Or as Lyotard himself explains it, we live in a culture in which "one listens to reggae, watches a western, eats McDonald's food for lunch and local cuisine for dinner, wears Paris perfume in Tokyo and 'retro' clothes in Hong Kong; knowledge is a matter of TV games."[71]

In contrast to Lyotard and although radical indeed, the remarkable speculations concerning simulation and reproduction put forward by Jean Baudrillard shed considerable light on our quest to understand the nature of the today's consumer culture. In his 1981 essay, "Simulacra and Simulations," Baudrillard postulates that our modern ability to mass produce exact copies of things, to create multiple images and simulations of the real world, has

---

[67] Steven Best and Douglas Kellner, *Postmodern Theory: Critical Interrogations* (New York: The Guilford Press, 1991), 166.

[68] Jean-François Lyotard, *The Postmodern Condition* (Minneapolis: University of Minnesota Press, 1984), 3.

[69] Best and Kellner, *Postmodern Theory*, 151.

[70] Best and Kellner, *Postmodern Theory*, 165.

[71] Lyotard, *Postmodern Condition*, 76.

destroyed our ability to distinguish between what is simulation and what is real—between what is true and what is false. But for Baudrillard, this is not just a matter of the real becoming confused with the copy. Indeed, Baudrillard goes so far as to say that we have reached the point where, at times, the copy precedes the original; that is, that the original is a pure fabrication of the system, and that through mass reproduction of this artificial creation the system creates the illusion of an original reality that never existed. In this way, according to Baudrillard, the creation and mass production of simulations and images has murdered reality, and we are left with only copies of copies for which there is no original. This is what Baudrillard calls "the hyperreal," "the generation by models of a real without origin on reality."[72]

As an example, Baudrillard offers us Disneyland, not only as a fantasy, but as a simulation of American life. He then reminds us that American life, Los Angeles for example, is itself not real either, it is only a creation of the system's ability to create images and simulations. Baudrillard's point is not just that Disneyland is several generations of copies away from what is real, but that, as an *obvious* copy, it subtly works to reinforce the notion that Los Angeles is real.

Although perhaps a little convoluted and certainly a bit over-the-top, such a notion can go a long way toward explaining the working of today's consumer culture. Certainly, Baudrillard's speculations revolve around the system's unrelenting and singular self-perpetuating compulsion to reproduce itself. Furthermore, these speculations lead us directly to the notion that the process makes blind slaves of us all, for it invisibly and painlessly robs us of the ability to identify what is authentic.

Given the radical nature of Baudrillard's conclusions, many have a difficult time with his ideas. Still, if we can look beyond his categorical predictions, and take only the essence of Baudrillard's thoughts without the apocalyptic ramifications he suggests, we can come away with useful insights regarding the current state of affairs. Surely, the mass production of copies and the creation of multiple simulations do not fully rob us of our ability to distinguish the imaginary from the real, and certainly discernible elements of the real are still all around us. Nonetheless, the mass creation of copies can work as Baudrillard suggests, not so much by destroying our sense of what is real, but by blurring the line between what is copy and what is original, or even by obscuring the true nature of the original. Either way, although the world may not become totally weightless as Baudrillard projects, it surely becomes a place of increased ambiguity. In this context, Baudrillard not only

---

[72] Jean Baudrillard, "Simulacra and Simulations" (1981), in Mark Poster, ed., *Jean Baudrillard, Selected Writings*, Stanford: Stanford University Press, 1988, 166-184.

helps us to understand how mass reproduction and simulation are driving forces in today's consumer culture, he also explains how the system works through its simulacra to hinder our ability to see through these simulations, to obscure that which is real from our vision, to deceive us—how, despite its unreality, consumer culture fascinates us, while at the same time it dupes and enslaves us.

* * * * *

The critique of Modernity stretches from Descartes to Derrida and beyond, and although the current consumer culture is a recent, late-modern, post-industrial, or perhaps even postmodern phenomenon, depending on one's point of view, its roots predate those the modern. Clearly, this "Brief History of Consumer Culture" is far from comprehensive, however, it is not the aim of this book to dwell in the past, nor is it to split the hairs of theory. This book seeks to explore a part of the popular culture as it lies before us in America today, seductive, intoxicating, opaque, hollow, fascinating, depthless. This historical overview, abbreviated as it may be, is intended to lay groundwork for these explorations.

CHAPTER THREE: REINVENTING OURSELVES IN THE MARKET-
PLACE

The Quest for Individual Style

As the industrial age plundered on through the last half of the nineteenth century and into the twentieth, the picture of Modernity painted by the pundits of the era became bleak indeed. Marx bemoaned the exploitation of the proletariat and Weber grumbled about the subjugation of life to "instrumental rationality" and the "iron cage" of bureaucratic alienation. The general fear arose that the price of material prosperity in the industrial age would be monotony, conformity, and the machine-like tedium of a grey, mass-produced world. Workers would be separated from the land, stripped of their tools, robbed of their identity, and transformed into mere mechanical appendages of the machines they operated. Exploited, oppressed, and alienated, new generations of faceless factory hands, clerks, and minor executives would be housed in bleak, cookie-cutter row-houses or in monotonous, suburban "little boxes" and pacified by narrow selections of cheap products and hollow, conformist diversions distinguished only by their repetitive sameness. Such was the view of the future presented by the critics of Modernity in the first half of the twentieth century. As it turns out, they could not have possibly been more wrong.

With the appearance of a mature consumer culture in America, all possibilities for a drab, monotonous, modern world of colorless drudgery and conformity were forever erased. Modern consumer culture is the complete antithesis of modern visions of monotonous drudgery. It assaults us with endless horizons of color, spectacle, and light; entices us with fabulous vistas of diversion, fascinating entertainments and illusions; and ensnares us in an ever-changing landscape of superficial variety and perceived choice. In contrast to the mass-consumption and conformist mentalities envisioned in the first part of the last century, today we find ourselves confronted with the illusion of overwhelming choice. The today's consumer culture blinds us with its bounty in spectacles of countless products available in endless variations and styles, in hundreds of highly focused TV channels, magazines, movies, and in the cyber-wonders of the Internet where the mere click of a mouse is our key to seemingly anything. Today's markets and media are not limited by consolidating efficiencies, they are endlessly expanded by highly specific and diverse segmentations. As Stuart and Elizabeth Ewen note in their insightful *Channels of Desire*, "Today there is no fashion; there are only *fashions.*" "No rules, only choices." [73]

As the number of choices flaunted by the media and the marketplace multiply, a bilious overflow of new goods and new symbols obscures the traditional symbolic hierarchy of goods associated with the old class preferences. Today's commodity choices go well beyond the early marketer's simple color-coded graph defining consumers by class and income group. More complex matrices, countless new identities, and minutely targeted consumer strategies obscure simple class-driven notions of conspicuous consumption. New market dynamics emerge as consumers seek, not so much to achieve upward social mobility by copying the consumption patterns and lifestyles of the upper classes, but more often to create vibrant new lifestyles of their own. In this atmosphere, class signifiers become confused. What is the meaning of a $500 Yves St. Laurent bag when one can buy a virtually identical copy for $20? Likewise, what does it mean when wealthy Park Avenue matrons develop a taste for faded jeans with holes in the knees, or when your broker gets a tattoo? Fashions become fragmented and move beyond fashion, beyond the collective mode. Style becomes personal, a unique voice of one's "individuality, self-expression, and stylistic self-consciousness." [74] With so many new symbols and meanings that can be attached to so many new products and diversions, "Everyone can be anyone." [75] Long-sacred fashion codes are violated in a dynamic that cuts across class and income boundaries and obliterates the traditional social hierarchy. Individuality, one of the early casualties of industrialization and modernization, is resurrected in the choice of one's car, clothes, home décor, leisure activities, food, musical tastes, TV viewing and reading habits, and so on, as each consumer seeks to

[73] Stuart Ewen and Elizabeth Ewen, *Channels of Desire* (New York: McGraw Hill, 1982), 249-51.
[74] Featherstone, *Consumer Culture and Postmodernism*, 83.
[75] Ewen and Ewen, *Channels of Desire*, 249-51.

mix and match the diverse arrays of commodity building blocks available to fashion a unique self. In the complex folds of modern consumer culture, one can construct a distinctive identity and color in that highly personal work of art that we today refer to as a lifestyle.

Amid our scrambles to convert all the myriad products available in today's consumer culture symbolically into unique forms of self-expression, the old social coordinates rapidly disappear. Blinded by an unstable profusion of information and an explosive proliferation of images, the deterministic relationship between culture and society teeters and shifts. Previously fixed and even rigid social divisions begin to blur and become irrelevant. [76] Although taste can still be read in class structure, such readings have become increasingly difficult.

Many observers hold that the vast new array of choices today available to American consumers is not a response to autonomous consumer demand for the diverse symbols and images employed to shore up personal identity and to create alternate lifestyles. Rather, many suggest, such diversity of industrial output is the result of new technology-driven techniques like "short-run batch production," more flexible machinery, new methods of niche marketing, and "just-in-time" inventory control. Undeniably, a new retail culture has evolved that has "fine-tuned its approach to selling in parallel with the now fine-tuned classifications of the discrete market segments it addresses."[77] Further, new forms of media and advertising have recently evolved to manipulate the marketplace in much more detailed and targeted ways. These forms include proliferation of specialized periodicals and journals, cable television, satellite broadcasting, more detailed consumer databases, the internet and so on. At the bottom of it all, we find the recurring question: does production drive consumption, or is it the other way around?

In any case, the era of mass-production appears to be over, and "new imperatives in advertising" today operate to "address the now divergent and highly segmented tastes, needs, and sensibilities of the modern marketplace."[78] Paramount among these sensibilities is the desire to create unique individual identities by individuals or small groups of consumers. Clearly this is an image-driven, stylistic desire that creates a much richer consumer dynamic, a dynamic that undoubtedly responds to complex forces some of which operate well outside of the system's well-known manipulations.

Let us consider for a moment the complexities of this kind of quest for individual style. When present-day consumer culture was in its infancy, back

---

[76] Featherstone, *Consumer Culture and Postmodernism*, 83.
[77] Lee, *Consumer Culture Reborn*, 115.
[78] Lee, *Consumer Culture Reborn*, 115.

in the era of conspicuous consumption and the "status symbol," conventional wisdom held that the rich wielded powerful influence over questions of style. After all, the aspiring classes sought to emulate the fashions of the rich. Still, as it turned out, the rich could only influence style; they could not control it. At that time, many questions of style were also thought to be mediated by so-called "cultural intermediaries,"[79] the trend setters of the day—fashion gurus, designers, celebrities, and so on. Still, in this period, the symbols attached to various commodities were relatively simple and straightforward, and they tended to organize themselves along class and income lines. As technology and the media mushroomed, commodity symbols became more complex, multi-layered, more specific. Products carried new meanings in addition to the meaning of status, meanings that in some cases were very deliberately at odds with the status system and the objectives of conspicuous consumption.[80] No longer just a reflection of class and income, the new symbolic meanings attached to the products were extended to include notions of time, place, trend, occupation, gender, values, ethnicity, lifestyle, and so on. In this increasingly chaotic atmosphere, it was not long before consumers began to attempt to attach their own symbols to certain products, symbols that they themselves designed to meet their own personal needs, symbols they would employ to point to and elaborate their own chosen individual lifestyles. At this juncture, shopping had become a cultural project to complete the self, and consumer culture had reached maturity.

The diverse symbolic meanings attached to products today are complex and often subtle, but a few concrete examples will help draw them out and to illuminate the process by which such meanings are created, multiplied, and sustained. Let us take as an example the luxury automobile, Mercedes Benz. At the panicle of the Mercedes line of products is the "S Class Maybeck" sedan. Starting at $198,000, this car, according to the manufacturer's promotional literature, is an "uncompromised" "legend," "the foremost luxury sedan in the world" representing the latest in "elegance," "performance" and "innovation." Indeed, it is through the production of "high-end" models like the "S-Class" sedan and the $500,000, 617 horsepower "SLR-Class McLaren" roadster that Mercedes Benz creates and maintains its "legend." These cars incorporate all the auto-maker's latest design innovations, safety features, engineering and electronic technologies, and driver amenities. As the company's ads inform us, these cars are truly the work of "craftsmen," presenting the consumer

---

[79] Pierre Bourdieu, *Distinction: A Social Critique of the Judgment of Taste* (London: Routledge, 1984).
[80] McCracken, *Culture and Consumption II*, 43.

with a "ceaseless rush" of "hand built" perfection and flaunting impeccable "handcrafted appointment." With all the craftsmanship, engineering, research, and development that goes into these cars and with the limited potential consumer demand for half-million-dollar automobiles, it is highly unlikely that Mercedes can make a profit on these cars at any price. So why build and market them? Because within these cars—both through advertising and through messages physically stamped into the design and production of each car itself—lie highly sophisticated symbolic meanings that are transferred all the way down the line to every car Mercedes makes. The "S-Class" Mercedes is not just a car; it is, in a very real sense, an ad, not only for itself but also and more importantly for the whole line of Mercedes Benz cars to which it is imagistically linked, including the popular, affordable, mass-produced "C-Class" line, which starts at $46,000. The "S-Class" autos create a powerful cultural identity for the Mercedes brand and for all its hallmarked products. In the process, the mass-produced, competitively priced "C-Class" vehicles are equated with everything the "S-Class" vehicles have come to mean metaphorically, and the "S-Class" cars are thus, in large part, paid for by proceeds from the sale of other products. In this respect, the extremely high-end luxury models are little more than pure advertisements, circulating only as promotional signs for the brand.

This works at several levels. First, the extraordinary "S-Class" cars confirm the myth of German engineering mastery and technical precision, and all Mercedes vehicles borrow from the reinforced luster of this ongoing mythology. So it is that the superior design, craftsmanship, and grace of the "S-Class" autos transfer the perception of "German-made" quality to the entire "C-Class" line. It can be no coincidence that when Daimler and Chrysler merged, Dr. Dieter Zetsche, the company's German CEO, became the TV spokesman for Dodge trucks. He extolled Dodge's new line of pickups in precise English adorned with a clipped but charming German accent. The message of these ads was this: the Germans possess the most refined technical skills in the world, and now the precise geniuses who make the Mercedes Benz are applying their genetically inborn engineering skills in a re-design of this robust and distinctly American line of trucks. However, the message of German technical know-how and time-honored Germanic traditions for precision and craftsmanship are not the only symbols the "S-Class" autos transfer to the larger Mercedes line. In America, there is also the notion that Europe is both the source and the current repository of Old-World traditions of artistic and cultural refinement, that Europe possesses an aesthetic tradition that is unmatched in this county. Thus, the Mercedes "S-Class" models symbolically are perceived by Americans to embody a unique European synthesis of Art and Science. Further, in America it is also widely believed that in Europe the old aristocracy survives. Accordingly, Mercedes Benz's advertising subtly attaches this notion to its super-expensive "S-Class" motorcars and then by inference to the entire Mercedes line. The resulting commodity-symbol conveys to Americans the massage that such vehicles are not just the choice of the rich; they are also the choice of elevated and refined aristocratic social classes that exist only in Europe, social classes that thrive only in the rarefied continental atmosphere high above the level playing fields of a less culturally sophisticated New World. Thus, the message becomes that driving a Mercedes brings one closer not only to German craftsmanship and to the old school, European, artistic mastery, but also to Old World nobility. At the same time, Mercedes Benz's promotional efforts along these lines have the effect of reinforcing, naturalizing, and even expanding the myths of German technical prowess and Old-World artistic refinement as well as sustaining various illusions regarding the Continental aristocracy and the structure of the attending European social order.

By itself, all this may appear to be too stodgy to appeal to trendy American consumers seeking to create unique, up-to-date, personal images and lifestyles. However, when combined with other, hipper, more uniquely American commodity-symbols, the overall effect can be dazzling. As Andrew Wernick has observed, "The mutual entanglement of promotional signs in one domain with those in another has become a pervasive feature of our whole produced symbolic world." [81] We can listen to rap music and wear a cowboy hat while driving down to the Tasty-Freeze in our SLR roadster displaying a license plate that reads, "Nuke the Whales."

While Mercedes Benz advertising relies on notions of European craftsmanship and refinement and is aimed primarily at stimulating conspicuous consumption, fueling our desires to emulate the wealthy and the socially elevated classes, Chevrolet's earlier ads for its "Silverado" line of pickup trucks tapped the rich homespun vein of ingrained American nationalism. The campaign was built around John Mellencamp's hit song, "This is Our Country." The ads were a hyper-patriotic lyrical and visual appeal to all that the United States of America stands for: liberty, equality, right thinking, abundance, and the attainability of American dream. Mellencamp's lyrics extolled standing up for "what is right" as well as knowing the place to "stand and fight." The song emblematizes the notion that in America there is "a dream for everyone." The breadth and scope of the historical American

---

[81] Andrew Wernick, *Promotional Culture: Advertising, Ideology, and Symbolic Expression* (London: SAGE Publications, 1991), 12.

experience unfolded in each thirty-second ad, as the rusty-voiced singer took us from sea to shining sea, "from the east coast to the west coast" and down a "Dixie highway." The chorus presented a patriotic prayer, that the "voice of freedom" might "ring out through this land," and concluded by binding us all together as American citizens with the anthematic conclusion, "this is our country."

In all of the ads in the series, while Mr. Mellencamp sang, we were treated to an emotional montage of patriotic nostalgia and iconic Americana including images of cowboys, American troops returning from war, Rosa Parks on the bus, the Apollo moon landing, Muhammad Ali in the ring, weary firefighters, Dale Earnhardt in his winning Chevrolet race car, Martin Luther King Jr., workers at Mount Rushmore, a high school football game, even fireworks on the Fourth of July. In almost every scene, we saw vintage Chevy trucks at work and at play functioning as an integral part of the American experience. As each ad concluded, the words, "Our Country, Our Truck" were superimposed on the screen. The clear, even shameless, inference was that buying a Chevy truck affirmed one's citizenship and emblematized one's faith in America—that a Chevy truck valorized all that America stands for, and conversely that the entire American experience valorizes each Chevy truck. The pickup truck became an American icon, and to it, the ads attached a rich nationalistic ideology: freedom, perseverance, work, family, faith, and so on. The symbolic meanings here are myriad and poignant, and although an obvious manipulation, the message is both entertaining and compelling. Through these ads, the Chevrolet Silverado was impregnated with a vast array of symbolic meanings that each individual consumer could do with as he or she wished.

Of course, as the manipulators of the culture industry are keenly aware, the creation of new symbols is a complex and difficult matter. Like new products, one can present new symbols in the marketplace but there is no guarantee that consumers will embrace them. While advertisers labor to create national mega-trends, "street styles" appear, and many are widely copied. So begins a conflict of sorts. The marketplace is suddenly filled with various individuals and groups, all striving to prove that the symbols and the products that they embrace, are *the* symbols and products—that is, that their chosen symbols and products constitute a new style. Conversely, on the cutting edge of all of this, the most radical trendsetters are constantly in search of the new, and accordingly in their constant quest for novelty and uniqueness, these self-styled cultural intermediaries are quick to reject anything that has become "the accepted style." As Georg Simmel noted way back in 1904, "As fashion spreads, it gradually goes to its doom."[82] For Simmel, fashion was a moving contradiction, an unceasing battle between the contradictory forces of "imitation and differentiation"[83] in which consumers sought at once to emulate those they admire and to distinguish themselves from their peers. This conflict is today accelerated in popular culture as it simultaneously wages wars of both differentiation and uniformity. These conflagrations are complicated by the fact that some consumers select and combine different products to articulate their own personal lifestyles without a thought as to how others might react, thus ignoring both differentiation and imitation. The result is a process that knows no boundaries, no limits, no conventions or rules, a "floating field of unstable signifiers"[84] colliding in a dynamic spectacle of image and illusion so complex, it seems to obscure any semblance of permanent, widely understood meaning.

Nonetheless, meanings are present, if not on a universal level, certainly individually or at the level of some segmented group consciousness. That is, meaning may not exist in the modern context of a world rationally moving toward some universally valid, single, truth (style), but meanings may emerge from a postmodern view of the world as a cauldron containing numerous local, provisional, or even temporary truths (styles). In the segmented postmodern view, we can clearly see the classic confrontations between differentiation and imitation. For example, when young people elect the style of wearing the bills of their caps to the back, the differentiating nature of the style is clear. This style sends an unequivocal message to the older generation (who find this "look" ridiculous) that young people choose to reject established conventions. On the other hand, as the style spreads throughout the youth culture and beyond to those who simply want to be perceived as "young-at-heart," the imitative nature of the style also becomes clear. In the end, the symbolic message carries a built-in contradiction, "Come, and be different like *all of us.*"

Emancipation and Consumer Culture

Some would argue that personal style and differentiation are good things, and that despite the contradiction, they point to the fact that within today's consumer culture, meaning does exist, and emancipating messages are being sent and understood, at least by some. Such an argument insists that the

---

[82] Georg Simmel, "Fashion," in *International Quarterly*, 10(1), October 1904, 130-155, reprinted in *American Journal of Sociology*, 62(6), May 1957, 541-558.
[83] David Frisby, "Georg Simmel: First Sociologist of Modernity" in *Theory, Culture, and Society* Vol. 2 No. 3, 1985.
[84] Featherstone, *Consumer Culture and Postmodernism*, 85.

critics of modernity can't have it both ways. They can't lament the anonymity and alienation of the modern age, criticizing its inhabitants for having become faceless, hollow automatons, while at the same time condemning them for seeking to fill the modern void by piecing together workable personal identities, even if these identities are found in the perceived depthlessness of popular culture.

The litany of the modern journey is all too familiar: the reduction of the worker to a faceless cog; the obliteration of the work ethic; the erosion of church, family, community and the other institutions that once supplied the self with meaning and identity; the shallowness of the media, of consumer society, and of popular culture. It is a sad tale, but is it universally true?

There are those who put a different spin on the modern loss of identity, those who theorize that our modern Western selves "are deliberately left blank so that individuals might exercise modern freedoms of choice."[85] In this fluid new age, we are each relatively free to personally define matters of gender, personality, lifestyle, and so on. This makes us eager consumers of the symbolic meanings contained in the goods we encounter every day.[86] This buoyant line of thought suggests that consumers are not necessarily manipulated, unwitting dupes of the culture industry, but autonomous actors able to make informed choices. In this view, consumers can take possession of the "bundles of meanings" available in the marketplace and intelligently put them to work to fashion workable new selves.[87] This more optimistic view holds that people do not always behave or live like "the masses," that the consumers, who wander the labyrinthine passageways of today's consumer culture, are not "an aggregation of alienated, one-dimensional persons whose only consciousness is false," and that their relationship to the system that enslaves them is not one of unwitting dupes.[88] Perhaps today's consumers are not all the passive recipients of commercially manipulated meanings. Perhaps some are "possessed of their own culturally constituted power of discrimination" and "entirely capable of judiciously selecting and manipulating the meanings of the marketplace."[89] Perhaps "homogenous, externally produced culture cannot be sold ready-made." Maybe culture simply does not work like that. Maybe "popular culture is made by people, not by the culture industry." [90]

---

[85] McCracken, *Culture and Consumption II*, 112.
[86] McCracken, *Culture and Consumption II*, 112.
[87] McCracken, *Culture and Consumption II*, 105.
[88] John Fisk, *Understanding Popular Culture* (London: Unwin Hyman, 1989), 23-4.
[89] McCracken, *Culture and Consumption II*, 44.
[90] Fisk, *Understanding Popular Culture*, 23-4.

In these thoughts, we find the beginnings of the notion that today's consumer culture might not exclusively be a mechanism of domination and enslavement but might also supply avenues of resistance to combat the abuses of the larger universal system of which it is a part. Some observers claim to have found a "marvelously subversive space"[91] submerged within the culture. Such claims insist that some commodities can be fashioned by consumers into "a bulwark against the status system," a "protection against the intrusions and demands of the designer, the marketer, the showy neighbor," and hammered into a type of utility that is "very deliberately at odds" with the manipulations of the system.[92] For example, many consumers create a kind of protection in their homes, or at least in one or two rooms in their homes. Realizing that once a purchase transaction is complete, a commodity's symbolism can be possessed and then altered, consumers can choose to ignore the meanings imposed by the culture industry and make the thing truly their own by attaching their own meanings. When it comes to products for the home, these meanings are sometimes altered to create a kind of shelter against the endless bombardments of style and fashion, trend and image. Such a "homey" creation constitutes a return to the simple comforts of the real, a personal refuge, a highly individualistic statement that flies in the face of the profusion of symbols, images, and illusions that emanate from modern consumer culture. Stripped of the meanings attached by the culture to certain home furnishings and decorations, these products are used to fashion a kind of personal rebellion, a home designed for family and human interaction, and not for status and style.

All of this represents a concerted attempt to rescue consumer culture from the wholly negative definition that it is so often afforded in Critical Theory and in various forms of Marxism in which popular pleasures are generally seen as the blinding opiates of false consciousness. In this liberating endeavor, we find in modern consumer culture specifically, and in the current popular culture in general, a series of "liberating and empowering cultural resources,"[93] "spaces for self-expression and cultural resistance to domination."[94] All of this suggests that somewhere deep inside the culture, we can find treasures that represent the failure of the current system to produce a uniform popular culture that is wholly consistent with the ideology of that system.

---

[91] Lee, *Consumer Culture Reborn*, 53.
[92] McCracken, *Culture and Consumption II*, 43.
[93] Lee, *Consumer Culture Reborn*, 53.
[94] Lee, *Consumer Culture Reborn*, 50.

Depthlessness and Atomization in Consumer Culture

Even if the modern consumer culture does contain emancipating resources and serviceable avenues of resistance, most observers would warn that such emancipation and resistance is of the shallowest variety. After all, the personal identities we create using the commodities, entertainments, and diversions that are available in the marketplace are fabricated, not with real products and real experiences but with symbols, simulations, and illusions—copies of copies that are often several generations away from the real. Any personal identity fashioned from such flimsy materials must itself be flimsy indeed. Any resistance built around images and illusions without substance must itself be without substance; or so the argument goes.

It is generally agreed that in the era before the emergence of our mature consumer culture, personal identity in America was constructed from much more solid stuff: from work, from the pride of achievement; from a defining sense of family, community, and nation; from robust spiritual and ideological elements. This is the modern view, and its seemingly ironclad logic appears to us obvious, given, natural. So seamless is the logic of Modernity that few pause to consider the fact that modern notions of work, community, and nation themselves constitute only ethereal ideologies involving their own symbols and illusions—symbols and illusions that are part of a modern system of values. Is it not possible to fashion a workable ideology around leisure instead of work, liberated consumption instead of the lean ascetic of self-denial inherent in Puritanical notions of the goodness found in thrift and rational sacrifice? Is it not possible that modern values and ideologies embracing nationalism, thrift, the work ethic, democracy, and science are themselves also hollow, enslaving fabrications of a system designed to accomplish the endless reproduction of itself, just as the ideologies embracing consumption and pleasure that are found in modern consumer culture are employed by the same system to achieve the same end? Is it possible that this culture only appears to be depthless because we can only judge it from a modern point of view using modern values? If we take a critical look at the world that we have created employing these modern values, values that we are told are the products of science and reason, are we not compelled to question the validity of these values, and to reexamine the perceived depthlessness of today's consumer culture and the values it embraces?

Most would agree that the images and meanings attached by the culture industry to the commodities and the experiences found in modern consumer culture are suspect—hollow manipulations creating illusions of status and gratifications designed to pacify and enslave. However, what of the images attached to these products by the consumer himself or herself, the images he or she uses to construct individual lifestyles, meaning, and personal identity? Might these images carry more weight? Might these symbols contain elements of emancipation and personal rebellion against the system that makes such subvert-able product-images available?

Perhaps, but even though today's consumer culture may appear to contain positive, emancipating possibilities for today's consumers, at the same time and in a most fundamental way it robs consumers of any chance to achieve the real power necessary to effect changes in the system. Consumer culture remains an enduring agent of our enslavement, because the very nature of creating a unique lifestyle through consumption is highly individual, especially when it comes to the autonomous creation of personal symbols and images. In a word, this kind of consumption is atomizing. It is driven by a discrete personal logic, a logic that answers to the individual's personal goals, needs, tastes, and agendas. Any rebellion that might arise from this kind of consumption is by nature a rebellion of only one. So it is that modern consumer culture ensures that we are doomed to act alone in a battle that we cannot hope to win without communal effort.

Mature consumer culture seeks only its own perpetual expansion, and the choices it offers us are only those that further its narrow goal. Although it allows us seemingly unlimited, material, individual choices, it carries us publicly, ecologically, and politically toward destinations that are not chosen by us. We can choose the color of our sweater or the model of our car or the shows we watch on TV, but we cannot choose our collective destiny, because today's consumer culture insulates us from any sense of community and smothers the resources necessary for collective action. The vast menu of choices that are available to us offers us only the illusion of choice. We consume this illusion, this abundance, as discrete economic individuals, reduced to discrete social, economic, and political atoms who individually support the agendas of the culture, not as connected players in any larger forward-thinking collective. Consumption in a competitive market does not bind us together, does not inspire feelings of rebellious connectedness, does not unite us and arm us with the kind of reforming power that is only available in unity. Quite the contrary, consumption—and the creation of individual identities based upon consumption—alienate us from any sense of a larger revolutionary whole of which we might become a part.[95]

---

[95] Andrew Bard Schmookler, *The Illusion of Choice* (Albany: The State University of New York, 1993), 301.

Domination and Consumer Culture

Thus, we do not choose our destiny; consumer culture chooses it for us. In a convincing illusion of choice, our real choices are controlled by the very nature of the system in which we make them. We are offered rich individual options that are exquisitely sensitive to our needs in some areas and virtually no option at all in other collectively vital areas.[96] We may select a new car from showrooms filled with the latest sporty models, but we effectively have no choices when it comes to the techniques employed to combat global warming.

The enormous power of the modern, capitalistic American marketplace that is reflected so vividly modern consumer culture pulls everything into its all-encompassing orbit. "The market tends to sweep up all other institutions, all the cultural forces, and reform them in its own image." [97] Everything becomes an adjunct to the market, and yet, thanks to the manipulations of today's consumer culture, the illusion remains one of complete freedom. Behind this illusion lies the irony that the sum of these free-market choices is a world in which no one is free, a world that no one would choose, a world controlled by an autonomous mechanism that is blind to the long-term consequences of its own actions. Dazzled by the abundance of the modern marketplace and the new sense of re-created individual identity we have purchased there, we plunder on. Oblivious to the runaway, self-perpetuating system that enfolds us, we remain locked in the tender embrace of a system that possesses no realistic perspective or sensitivity regarding social justice, war, human exploitation, or the fragility of the natural world in which it exists. Our politicians may pay lip service to these issues, but at the end of the day, they are only puppets, chosen and controlled by a system that understands the value of creating illusions, including the illusion that these issues are being addressed.

In all of this, the total domination exercised by the market system is effectively hidden from our view. Our vibrant consumer culture obscures the market's control with blinding material fascinations and at the same time, the system disseminates the powerful myth of the "free market," continually subjecting us to thorough ideological brainwashing. The result is an idolatry of the material centered in the sacred and unassailable dogma of the "invisible hand of competition." Around this holy catechism, America is creating a new value system aimed at the perpetuation of a radically new logic: the adoration of the commodity, the worship of celebrity and success, the enshrinement of wealth, and the perpetual expansion of the economic

---

[96] Schmookler, *The Illusion of Choice*, 11-12.
[97] Schmookler, *The Illusion of Choice*, 71.

sphere.[98] At the center of this evolving new creed lies the notion that human well-being is measured first and foremost in material terms, and that human fulfillment springs not from achievement and work but from the knowledge of how to spend and enjoy. This is to say, not from production but from consumption. Once baptized into this cult of the material, we enter the cathedrals of the marketplace, and we are born again in the myriad identity choices we find there. But there is no power in such a conversion. Like all conversions, this one springs from a personal relationship with our new God. In the cult of the commodity, there can be no sense of congregation, no community of souls. Unlike the old American deities that united us in a consensus of liberty, opportunity, and hard work, the new commodity-God seeks communion only with the individual. No fellowship of believers can be tolerated, for the commodity-God knows that in the collective there is power. The commodity-God knows that the collective will spawn heresies, common concerns, blasphemies against the rigid doctrines of consumption and economic growth, concerns for the bio-system, concerns for the impoverished, concerns for a world at war. Such heresies are not tolerated in the cathedrals of modern consumer culture.

---

[98] Schmookler, *The Illusion of Choice,* 145.

CHAPTER FOUR: MEDIA CULTURE

Television: Creating Model Citizens

At the very heart of American popular culture lies the vast technological wonderland of contemporary American media; and at the heart of today's all-engrossing media culture lies television, one of consumer culture's most able henchmen. In an impossibly complex, evolving spectacle of images and effects, modern television hopelessly blends the realms of art, popular culture, news, history, fantasy, and ideology into a stupefying profusion of escapist entertainments designed to endlessly perpetuate the world of the commodity. Viewers are first seduced and then addicted. Before television's glowing alter, they fashion new identities, immersing themselves in fantasies and dreams that mold behavior and thought.[99] Wielding television like an invincible weapon, today's consumer culture wages a "permanent opium war"[100] that intoxicates and subdues, blinding pacified viewers to the need for resistance.

Television as an addictive drug is a familiar metaphor, voiced not only as a serious real-world concern but also in science fiction and in myriad academic critiques of the technical age. Some observers of the popular culture charge that, like all addictions, television leads its victims to "harder stuff," luring viewers in the direction of the ultimate addiction, the unbridled consumption of commodities. Like all the spectacles in today's consumer culture, television atomizes viewers. Its one-way nature cuts off collective options and presents

---

[99] Douglas Kellner, "Media Culture and the Triumph of the Spectacle," in Geoff King, ed., *The Spectacle of the Real: From Hollywood to Reality TV and Beyond* (Bristol, UK: Intellect, 2005), 22.
[100] Guy DeBord, "Thesis Number 44," in *The Society of the Spectacle* (Detroit: Black and Red, 1967), quoted in Kellner, "Media Culture," 25.

each viewer individually with a vast selection of goods and lifestyles from which he or she can personally choose to experience even more intoxicating satisfactions. Such critics insist that, on television, "Everything that was real is moved away into representation,"[101] and that, as viewers, we no longer experience reality, because television presents us with a world of "pervasive separation," in which our traditional families and communities dissolve and are replaced by the illusory families and communities that we see on the screen.[102] As with drugs, the satisfactions derived from "normal," real-world experiences are overwhelmed and eventually replaced by new, more powerful, fabricated experiences that beget new needs for the increasingly heightened hyper-reality that we can only access through illusions available in today's consumer culture. Thus, television creates ravenous consumers of illusions[103] and in so doing, it creates model citizens of the new culture of Consumerism. It is by this mechanism that this new culture perpetually expands its dominion. With the help of television advertising, the desire for one product is continually displaced onto the next product, then the next, in an addiction that differs from narcotics only in the fact that it completely hides its existence beneath the system's seemingly rational economic structure. Like consumer culture itself, television's bias is veiled from our view, and through the power, variety, and preponderance of its presentations, it naturalizes its manipulated view of the world into a "given," "taken-for-granted" reality.[104] In the world of consumer culture, "To view is to surrender."[105]

The post modernist thinker Jean Baudrillard takes this idea even farther. For Baudrillard, television is the "triumph of the signifying culture," a world of simulation and cultural disorder completely saturated with signs, meanings, and messages. According to him, television constitutes "a simulational world in which the proliferation of signs and images has effaced the distinction between the real and the imaginary"[106] and created "a depthless aestheticized hallucination."[107] In the impossibly complex tangles of televised images that parade across the screen, Baudrillard sees a kind of cultural rupture in which signs break free from their referents and become unstable, free floating signifiers, in a chaotic world of "pastiche, eclectic mixing of codes,

---

[101] DeBord, *The Society of the Spectacle*, Thesis Number 1.
[102] Scott Bukatman, "Who Programs You? The Science Fiction of the Spectacle," in Peter Brooker and Will Brooker, ed., *Postmodern Afterimages: A Reader in Film, Television, and Video* (London: Arnold, 1997), 75.
[103] DeBord, *The Society of the Spectacle*, Thesis Number 47.
[104] Glen Creeber, ed. *Tele-visions: An Introduction to Studying Television* (BFI: London, 2006), 48.
[105] Scott Bukatman, "Who Programs You?" 75-6.
[106] Featherstone, *Consumer Culture and Postmodernism*, 85.
[107] Featherstone, *Consumer Culture and Postmodernism*, 55.

bizarre juxtapositions, and unchained signifiers, which defy meaning and readability."[108] The result, according to him, is a kind of "nihilism of the sign" [109] that dominates the present age of consumer culture.

Such readings are radical indeed, and they seem to deny previous critiques of television as a modern homogenizing force, a purveyor of uniformity and conformity. Nonetheless, and despite Baudrillard's insistence that the media fragments symbolic meanings, in the broadest sense television still presents something of a unity as it works to endlessly perpetuate the diverse world of the commodity. With its focus on style and fashion, it hypes the latest trend and insidiously replaces local and regional tastes, mannerisms, and individualistic patterns of thought with uniform, institutionalized models that have powerful homogenizing effects. In addition, Baudrillard's extreme views seem to largely discount any positive cultural value television may have to offer in areas like education, information, edification, the presentation of positive identity models, and so forth. Nonetheless, we can all point to individual programs that uplift, educate, stimulate debate, and even provoke positive action, and yet at the same time we must admit that, taken as a whole, the world of television does seem to fit at least some aspects of Jean Baudrillard's radical vision. MTV alone might prove the point, but more generally Baudrillard's insights can be difficult to reconcile at the level of the individual program. They do, however, make sense if we simultaneously consider the television world in its entirety, and indeed, all of us quite frequently do exactly that, not only mentally but also physically. For example, all of us "channel hop." We may tell ourselves that we are searching for something interesting to watch, but in truth, "channel hopping" has become a form of entertainment in and of itself. We mindlessly flip through the hundreds of channels available on cable and satellite TV. We wander in the labyrinthine menus of scores of streaming services. Here is a touchdown, here a salmon mousse; here a man is killed; here trout swim upstream to spawn. Our minds become saturated with images. Which ones deserve our attention? Which should we ignore? The saturation of symbols and meanings is far too great for us to absorb, and in the end there can only be either equivalence or meaninglessness. Baudrillard's confounding prose is simply an attempt to imply that, over time, through television, consumer culture creates in our minds an indecipherable collage of symbols and images. On television, we constantly encounter a moving, expanding, changing flow of images, information, ideas, and data that eventually overwhelms us in its complexity, a complexity that is infinitely multiplied by the changing

---

[108] Featherstone, *Consumer Culture and Postmodernism*, 20.
[109] Featherstone, *Consumer Culture and Postmodernism*, 55.

content that each image carries with it and by these image's free-flowing contextual relationship one to the other. Taken as a whole, television is a numbing spectacle, a powerful hallucinogen that can trivialize the sacred and give importance to the banal, an opiate that sucks us into the gleaming black hole and leads us eventually to the neon palaces of the commodity. Television is not selective. It levels society. Engrossing everything in its path, it is easily the most powerful democratizing force in history. Television is to modern consumer culture what the chain saw was to the timber industry.

The broad sweep of television's aggregate complexity notwithstanding, it is also possible to reconcile Baudrillard's radical visions at the level of the individual program. No matter how realistic or how fantastic it may attempt to be, television places its unique mark on everything, branding every realistic offering with the indelible mark of entertainment, fantasy, and spectacle, and at the same time incorporating the real into every fiction. In the end, the proliferation of signs and meanings becomes so complex that we are unable to distinguish between fact and fantasy, between the real and the imaginary, between truth and untruth. Take, for example, television's presentation of war, either as news or as fictional drama. Those who have been in battle will tell you that the true nature of war consists of seemingly interminable periods of abject boredom punctuated by brief moments of sheer terror. Television presents us only with pyrotechnic spectacles of terror and death, leaving out the endless tedium, because it "just does not make for good television." As a result, TV war presents only selective, spectacular, symbolic keyhole views of a much larger event. In another example, dramatic story lines are "ripped from the headlines" to create fictional "docu-dramas" that muddy the waters separating fiction from fact. The examples are endless. Hard news is skewed to emphasize the spectacular, live sporting events become impossible extravaganzas of celebrity and graphic effects, history is fictionalized, and drama and fantasy are infused with factual events and real-life characters. Over top of it all, television spreads its blinding gloss of special effects, glittering graphic overlay, neon set design, and editorial flare. Before our very eyes, representations of the real slowly evolve into manipulations of the real. Reality melts away and becomes fantasy and fantasy melts away and becomes real. TV dissolves into real life and real life dissolves into TV until, in the end, television becomes reality and reality becomes something less than television, a remnant, "the usurpation of the real by its own representation."[110] All the while, commodities relinquish their utility as they are themselves transformed into fantasies, symbols, and

---

[110] Bukatman, "Who Programs You?" 80.

entertainments. The distinction between the ad and the program is blurred and finally disappears.

The escapist nature of American television cannot be overstated. It is tireless in its search for the new, for variety, for expanded landscapes in which viewers might lose themselves in their search for gratification, hope, release, identity and self-esteem. Like a giant lottery, TV's manipulations are at once compelling and transparent. Anyone might win the prize, and yet everyone knows that the odds against such a win are astronomically poor. Nonetheless, just as scores of contestants win daily on TV quiz shows, we are all invited to picture ourselves as the winner of millions. Just as TV celebrities live glamorous fantasy lives, we are all invited to picture ourselves in the starring role, accepting the Emmy, saving the town, winning the girl, making the winning last-second touchdown. As Max Horkheimer and Theodor Adorno remind us, "The starlet is meant to symbolize the typist. The girls in the audience all feel they could be on the screen, and yet all realize how infinitesimal such a chance actually is."[111] Such is TV's promise, a possibility so remote as to be false, and yet it nonetheless entices, stupefies, and sedates us all. And once enticed and stupefied, we are all offered the more immediate gratifications attainable in the consumer culture. We are told that we can get anything we want. Stressing credit cards and new lines of credit, TV urges us to buy whatever we want, whenever we want it, to "turn a deferred future into an immediate present,"[112] to buy into larger commodity lottery in which the prize is the same sense of personal identity and self-esteem that the stars we all hope to become enjoy on TV. Television's clear and unequivocal message is this: the commodities so readily available to us offer the same glamorous lifestyles we see on the screen. Accepting the promise of television's audacious message, we live lives of utter sedation dominated by the seamless, automatic ability of the system to replicate and expand itself by employing powerful psychological machinery that is beyond the control of anyone.

Television's Brief Journey from the Real to the Unreal

Like so many agents of today's consumer culture, American television manifests a fundamental irony: the medium that began its life as a kind of "witness to reality," quickly evolved into the medium most adroit at manipulating the real. As we have already noted, TV's transformation began in the early 1960s with the proliferation of color programs, a breakthrough that

---

[111] Adorno and Horkheimer, "The Culture Industry," 16.
[112] Umphlett, *From Television to the Internet*, 83.

was quickly followed by the perfection of videotape and a vast array of other technological advances aimed at the transferal, storage, and manipulation of televised sounds and images. The shift in popular programming that took place in the mid-1960s clearly exemplifies TV's movement away from its early flat, realistic landscape of programs in favor of more fantastic horizons. In this period, the primarily "live" presentations of Ed Sullivan, Jackie Gleason, Sid Caesar, and Milton Berle began to disappear, and the popularity of realistically set dramas like *Gunsmoke*, *Dragnet*, and *Perry Mason* began to wane. In their place, the viewing public of the mid-60s embraced a new generation of wild fantasy-based offerings like *The Man From U.N.C.L.E.* (1964), *Flipper* (1964), *Gilligan's Island* (1964), *The Munsters* (1964), *The Wild, Wild West* (1965), *Star Trek* (1966), and *Batman* (1966).

By the early 1970s, television's "live," documentary orientation had all but disappeared, replaced by an increasingly spectacular focus on the fantastic. Born as the children of a seemingly reliable purveyor of faithful representations of events and programs broadcast as they occurred, television's unedited, early offspring would add credibility to the medium's later progeny of manipulated, enhanced visual illusions. Television had become a sorcerer, well-versed in the twin arts of making fantasies real and making the real fantastic, a wizard whose dual magic was at the same time wholly credible and totally incredible and whose primary potion was no longer the unedited word but the enhanced image. The medium that had begun by showing us "history in the making" had developed a style so audacious as to color, manipulate, and even create much of the history it revealed—a new kind of shocking, self-reflective, temporary, "televisionized" history that was simultaneously real and fabricated, both legitimate and suspect. The medium that had been characterized as a "vast wasteland"[113] by the chairman of the FCC in 1961 soon developed a flashy, multi-foliate style so self-conscious and diverse as to become the gleaming popular culture it purported to reflect. To paraphrase Jean Baudrillard, television offers us "an aesthetic which is inseparable from its own structure," a reality that has become "confused with its own image."[114] As with all of consumer culture's transformations, the drab, empty "wasteland" of early modern electronic communications had become an escapist wonderland of color, fantasy, and illusion, the unrivaled and seminal voice of the blinding new world of the commodity.

As television followed its seemingly preordained progression from the real to the unreal, from the flat comic reality of *I Love Lucy* to the whimsical

---

[113] Newton Minow, "Television and the Public Interest," in Lester Thonssen, *Representative American Speeches 1961-1962* (New York The H. W. Wilson Company, 1962).
[114] Jean Baudrillard, *Simulations* (New York: Semiotext, 1983), 151.

fantasy of *Mister Ed* to the outlandish visual exaggerations of *Ally McBeal*, America became a nation of captivated viewers, a nation that was watching and could not look away. The rest of the world was soon to follow. Meanwhile, the visual immediacy of television's allure turned news into sensationalist entertainment, molded public affairs and politics into vaudevillian theater, transformed sports into spectacles of cult-like fascination, and created a torrent of instant celebrity. Even advertising became part of the show, as thirty-second spots evolved into mini-dramas and micro jokes, and the commodities that these spots promoted, themselves, became the featured entertainers of the consumer culture.

The camera, that unblinking eyewitness to the modern scene, soon developed the capacity to exploit compelling theatrical elements in everything. In an early example, the world witnessed the "live" assassination of Lee Harvey Oswald on TV, and those images set in motion a gripping, self-perpetuating, symbolic drama of conspiracy, intrigue, and innuendo that would be re-broadcast, re-evaluated, and re-lived without end. Only television could have created such a circus, and today it seems television expands almost every event in a similar mini-tempest of dramatic symbolism, speculation, half-truth, implication, and doubt. Such storms of intrigue are not simply the product of commercialized tabloid television news, they are the result of the entire medium's remarkable ability to both fanaticize reality and to make the fantastic seem real, and then to exploit the fascinating misty netherworld in between.

So it is that television creates a world that is somewhere in between fantasy and reality, a world that is neither wholly real nor wholly imagined. In this world, signs begin to multiply their meanings, and news and history become entertainments. Here is a world to which we can escape and attempt to reconstruct our lost identities. This reality/fantasy netherworld of today's consumer culture as portrayed on television offers us "release, freedom, transport, and escape," providing intoxications characterized by the "sheer mindless pleasure of emancipation from reason, from responsibility, from tradition, from class, and from all other bonds that restrain the self."[115] In this escapist world, information and entertainment—reality and fantasy—are hopelessly blended, and the resulting product is neither fully real nor fully illusory. *Survivor* is not "reality TV"; it is a staged creation of reality. *Law and Order* is not always a fictional drama; it is often a dramatization of real-world events.

---

[115] Neal Gabler, *Life the Movie: How Entertainment Conquered Reality* (New York, Knopf, 1998), 205.

The deeper irony of television's transformation from a representation of the real world to a reality/fantasy netherworld is that no one is really duped. In an odd paradox of perception, we demand more and more fantasy while at the same time we become increasingly aware and skeptical of the media's growing abilities to digitally manipulate its content. Everyone recognizes special effects for what they are and a re-enactment for what it is; and everyone knows that a touchdown is just a touchdown no matter how many angles are employed to examine it—no matter how many bands play, and cheerleaders cheer, and fans go crazy. The deeper irony is that, despite the fact that we see through its trickery, we allow ourselves to become immersed in this trickery. We somehow cannot do otherwise. Ours is not simply the cynicism of one who sees the wires in the magic show; ours is the sadder cynicism of seeing the wires, and having realized the trick, choosing to believe in the magic anyway. Through television, today's consumer culture has manipulated our perceptions to the point where it no longer needs to hide its manipulations. We are aware that the commodity-Gods that we worship are false Gods, and yet we choose to worship Them anyway, because They are seemingly the only Gods available these days.

Television, Media Culture, and Consumer Culture

Walter Benjamin argued that movies, along with modern media, the marketplace, and even the city, represented an industrially reproduced illusion, where "art and reality had switched places."[116] For Benjamin, the modern urban world was "an artificial landscape as totally encompassing as the earlier natural one."[117] Writing two decades before television, Benjamin insisted that the mass media, especially film, replicated the commodity world endlessly; still he postulated that film had the potential to be used in a critical way, not to reproduce illusions of modernity, but to point to the fact that the modern world was an illusion. Thus, quite early on, Walter Benjamin recognized the power of film and modern media, first as a weapon used to create and reproduce the illusions that characterized the expanding world of the commodity, but also as a weapon that could be used to dispel such illusions.

Back in the 1940s, when television was in its technological infancy, film was the undisputed arch-henchman of our emerging consumer culture. At that time, Max Horkheimer and Theodor Adorno saw film as the "triumph of invested capital" and the "absolute master" in the culture industry. Film,

---

[116] Susan Buck-Moss, "Benjamin's *Passagen-Werk*," *New German Critique*, No. 29,1983, 213.
[117] Featherstone, *Consumer Culture and Postmodernism*, 73-4.

these insightful critical theorists opined, represented "the fusion of all the arts in one work," the "alliance of word, image and music" reflecting the total "surface of social reality." Nonetheless, at the same time they accurately predicted television's triumph, predicting that its impact would be "quite enormous" and that TV's proliferation would "intensify the impoverishment of aesthetic matter so drastically that by tomorrow the thinly veiled identity of all industrial culture products can come triumphantly out into the open."[118] In other words, they prophesied an illusion so enticing, so compelling, indeed so seemingly real, that it would soon outgrow the need to hide the fact that it was an illusion.

Horkheimer and Adorno were not alone. There were many in the 1930s and 40s who predicted the coming power of television to dominate modern life, and in the early 1950s, it was thought that the emergence of TV into an American marketplace dominated by film and radio would result in a notable clash between the brash electronic new-comer and the crafty old masters. As TV hit the market, observers settled back to watch a bloody turf war within the culture industry, but after a few opening skirmishes the hostilities were called off and a powerful alliance ensued. By the early 1960s it had become clear that TV was adroit at promoting movies and that movies were supplying TV with endless hours of rich, diverse, engaging program material. The two great media giants that had appeared destined to clash in all-out war had quickly become devoted brothers and cooperative lieutenants in the service of modern consumer culture while radio jettisoned flashy variety, adventure, and crime shows, ditched sitcoms, and returned to its roots in news and music.

Very early on, it became clear that television would usurp radio's claim to the dramas and variety shows that radio had pioneered. In fact, many of TV's earliest shows were structured by copying earlier radio formats, and many, like *Dragnet*, *The Lone Ranger*, and *Sergeant Preston of the Yukon*, were direct TV adaptations of ongoing successful radios shows. Similarly, radio's approach to variety entertainment with its vaudevillian roots, was appropriated for TV in the work of such early luminaries as Ed Sullivan, Milton Berle, Sid Caesar, Jackie Gleason, and Dinah Shore. In the face of television's success, radio was forced to return to its roots in news and music, filling the hours with on-site newscasts, call-in tabloid, talk shows, endless commentary, and a rapidly splintering array of formatted music broadcasts, catering to pop, nostalgia, R&B, country, and the emerging genre of rock and roll. In another of its remarkable transformations, modern consumer culture had turned the

---

[118] Horkheimer and Adorno, "The Culture Industry," 6.

playing of a song into an advertisement for that song, and had cast a new radio personality called the disc jockey as a fast-talking salesman.

Thirty years later, the appearance of the music video would further escalate the blurring of the distinction between program and ad at the very time when musical genre distinctions themselves were becoming smeared and blended by increased listener eclecticism and the media-produced phenomenon called "cross-over." By this time, netherworlds of image and style had become familiar cultural furniture: fine art had blended with commercial graphics, the avant-garde had become infused with kitsch, and literature had cross-bred with pulp fiction. As was already the case with radio, where records were both program and promotion at the same time, music videos also exhibited the characteristics of both entertainments and ads. In addition, the new music-video form appropriated elements from myriad other cultural forms: opera, dance, television, animation, fashion, and live performance. Again, consumer culture was blurring the lines. News had become entertainment, and the entertainment world had become news; art and popular culture had merged; and music had ceased to be just an art and had become both a commodity and an advertisement for itself.

While television was changing the face of American radio, it was also precipitating notable changes in the world of film. Even though television at first seemed a crass and comparatively crude curiosity, and although film had begun to garner the status of a legitimate art form, it was still clear from the beginning that TV posed a threat to the film industry and that the day would come when this artistic credibility gap would begin to disappear. After all, both television and film sought to exploit the modern world's need to escape, to reconstruct damaged personal identities, and to find new meaning in a seemingly chaotic world. Both offered viewers a more immediate way to perceive the real world, and at the same time, an accessible way to escape from it. Indeed, television's escape route was clearly more accessible. Thus, since it seemed certain that TV would diminish film's eminence, the cinematic world quickly moved to call attention to early television's patent limitations. With its small black and white screen, tiny speaker, fuzzy reception, and limited choice of program material, television at first appeared no match for the colorful spectacle of the big screen, theater sound systems, and the wide diversity of films from which the public could choose. Nonetheless, in response to TV's potential, the movie industry set about redoubling its efforts to do what it did best: to create spectacle and fantasy.

Certainly, in 1950, the creation of spectacle and fantasy was no stranger to the film industry. *Gone with the Wind* and *The Wizard of Oz* dated from the late 1930s, as did feature animation and increasingly adroit special effects techniques. In response to television's initial allure, 1950s movie theater audiences were treated to cinematic spectacles of Broadway musicals brought to the screen in flashy productions that were well beyond the technological capability of the infant TV industry. At the big studios, emphasis shifted from producing large numbers of film releases catering to movie-goers' voracious appetites for variety, to producing panoramic, epic films like *The Robe* (1953), *The Ten Commandments* (1956), and *Ben Hur* (1959). The 1960s saw this trend continue with releases like *Lawrence of Arabia* (1962) and *Doctor Zhivago* (1965). Meanwhile more spectacular film presentation technologies emerged with the development of Cinemascope, Cinerama, 70mm and wide screen equipment, and surround sound. As the 1970s began, the movie industry took advantage of a more permissive cultural climate to exploit themes of explicit sex and spectacular violence, themes that have continued to characterize the "blockbuster" hits of today. At the same time, films began to explore the social and political issues of the day, taking graphic looks at war, crime, and the seamy underside of society.

Despite the film industry's efforts to outdo television with sweeping epics, more spectacular theater presentations, and graphic displays of sex, violence, and the darker corners of modern life, the forces binding the film industry to the television industry continued to increase. It became increasingly clear that the movies needed television to promote the new, more expensive productions, and to supply after-markets for old films. Television in turn became an enormously successful purveyor of old movies. By the 1980s, Disney, Fox, MGM, Universal and the other large studios had bought heavily into TV, just as CBS, NBC, ABC, and Turner bought heavily into the movies. Consumer culture had completed another of its transformations. The marriage of film and television created a seamless world of spectacular images, stereophonic sounds, glamorous celebrities, changing fashion, flashy trend, and shifting symbols dedicated to the reproduction, regeneration and perpetuation of the commodity. In this glossy new world, the distinction between programming and marketing soon became impossibly blurred. New film releases fascinated throngs of awed viewers constructing new worlds of fantasy and rendering the real fantastic while at the same time, creating new fashions, new lines of products, and countless endorsements and product exposures associated with each film. Video then turned the film itself into a new kind of commodity, and finally television aired the film over and over, embedding stars, themes, images, fashions, and associated commodities deeper and deeper into the public consciousness.

Perhaps the best example of the marriage of TV and film and the resulting blurring of programming and marketing is *Star Wars*. George Lucas' six-part epic of galaxies at war is paradigmatic of film fantasy, special effects, and spectacle, and its success not only wowed theater audiences, sold millions of videos, and pimped countless products on TV, it also begot a new universe of games, toys, posters, and T-shirts. The licensing of new *Star Wars* products and images eventually seemed to out-shine the film itself. With the help of television, Lucas's films themselves slowly became little more than advertisements for the wide array of products that they had inspired and for the myriad brands that their producers had endorsed. At the same time, these products and endorsements became ads for the film. In a sweeping illusion of space and war, good and evil, *Star Wars* had blended film and television, marketing and programming, fantasy and everyday life into a vast commodity world all its own. The Force was indeed with us, and the Force was the commodity and its attending consumer culture.

Star Wars is certainly not the only example. Most successful motion pictures and television shows beget marketing endorsements, cross-promotional schemes, and even product lines all their own. One need only open any catalogue to be assaulted with the evidence. The 2007 Toys R Us Christmas catalogue, for example, flaunts a WWE (World Wrestling Enterprises) "Money in the Bank Ladder Match Set," a *Pixar Cars* (the motion picture) "Mountain Challenge Play Set," and a *Hannah Montana* acoustic guitar on the very first page. Elsewhere in the catalogue one finds *Thomas Train*, *Power Rangers*, *Spiderman*, and *Bratz* paraphernalia, all manner of toys with Walt Disney character tie-ins, as well as a "*CSI* Investigation Kit," a *Harry Potter* game, and an "*American Idol* Challenge Set" complete with a tiny microphone.

The list is endless, and the message is clear. Consumer culture begins its indoctrination of its future followers at a very young age. According to sociologist, Juliet Schor, today the average 10-year-old has memorized about 400 brands, the average kindergartner can identify some 300 logos, and from as early as age two kids are "bonded to brands."[119] As these youngsters grow, they become accustomed to a world in which art, everyday life, ads, movies, radio, TV shows, commodities, displays, and marketing schemes, and spectacles of all sorts blend and intermingle until it is impossible to distinguish where one leaves off and the other begins. In the world of modern consumer culture, nothing is ordinary; everything is touched by spectacle and fantasy; and the ubiquitous invitation to consume permeates everything and becomes indistinguishable not only from art and entertainment but also from the most commonplace elements of everyday life.

---

[119] Juliet B. Schor, *Born to Buy: The Commercialized Child and the New Consumer Culture* (New York: Schribner, 2005), 20, 25.

Many thinkers believe that it is through this blurring of reality and fantasy that consumer culture masks its real agenda: the creation and reproduction of political and social ideologies and institutions that are conducive to its operations and expansions. Or as the Marxists would say, this is how capitalism hides the real social relations inherent in modern production, creates a pervasive false consciousness, and reinforces and naturalizes the dominate ideologies of capitalism. Nonetheless, there are others who insist that things are not that simple and that the effects of television and the mass-media cannot be "reduced to the materialization of a dominate ideology," that in fact, the modern American media still presents "occasions for subversive reworkings of a dominant ideology." This line of thought insists that TV and the other forces employed by today's consumer culture to seduce us and manipulate our thoughts have not fully secured an "ideological closure," have not in all cases "engaged us beyond our consciousness" in their quest to reproduce the dominate ideology of capitalism. Indeed, many still believe that the complexity and depth of the various signs and meanings that television delivers present us with something like a "menu" of ideological choices. At the bottom of this view is the larger conclusion that popular culture and even consumer goods, themselves, might, at least in some instances, offer "liberating experiences" and create "empowering cultural resources."[120]

---

[120] Lee, *Consumer Culture Reborn*, 52-53; Fiske, *Understanding Popular Culture*, 23-4.

Chapter Five: Virtual Reality and Consumer Culture

Cyberculture, Simulation, and Consumer Culture

Nothing better illustrates the totality of American consumer culture's blinding aesthetic hyper-reality than today's growing cyber-world of interlaced computer technology: that unstable, often playful world of artificial stimulation, symbolic imagery, and pure information and disinformation. In his later writings, Jean Baudrillard, himself, is quick to expound on the coincidence of virtual reality and his earlier notions of hyper-reality. Calling the virtual world "more complete," than the world of simulation and simulacrum, Baudrillard postulates that, because of its perfection and its completeness, this "perfectly homogenized, digitized and operationalized" world is actually a substitute for hyper-reality.[121] In his recent writings, Baudrillard waxes almost poetic concerning the virtual world, calling it "the final phase of this enterprise of simulation," "the perfect crime," a "total substitution of the world," the "cloning of reality and the extermination of the real by its double," "the highest stage of simulation," and "the stage of the final solution by the volatilization of the world's substance into an immaterial realm and a set of strategic calculations."[122] In all this, Baudrillard insists that virtual reality constitutes something radically beyond even the hyper-real's fantastic "aesthetic hallucination." For Baudrillard virtual reality represents

---

[121] Jean Baudrillard, *Passwords* (London and New York: Verso, 2003), 39.
[122] Jean Baudrillard, *The Intelligence of Evil or the Lucidity Pact* (Oxford: Berg, 2005), 27, 34, 44; Jean Baudrillard, *The Perfect Crime* (London and New York: Verso, 1996), 25.

the "unconditional realization of the world by the actualization of all data,"[123] an actualization that "puts an end to both reality and illusion."[124]

Within his discussions of the virtual world, we get the feeling that Baudrillard may not have originally been totally serious when he first expounded his notions of hyper-reality, that perhaps he initially meant his speculations to serve as something more like a provocation than anything else. However, the recent advance of digital technology into the world of everyday life seems to have convinced Baudrillard that events might be proving his wild notions right after all. In one memorable text, he confesses to "not really believing in it (the simulacrum), even hoping that the real will refute it," and to being "disarmed by the lamentable confirmation of...(his) words by an unscrupulous reality."[125]

In the popular culture, much has been made of the endless simulations and fascinations of the virtual world. Notions of "Cyborgs" and "The Matrix" have captured not only the popular imagination but have also clawed their way into the hallowed bastions of serious social theory and philosophy. Certainly, no one really believes that our bodies are imprisoned in individual incubators to supply power to a Matrix-like force that controls a real world we no longer consciously inhabit. Nonetheless, the existence of an indoctrinating dream-world where we, at least occasionally and perhaps metaphorically, relinquish of our subjectivity and surrender our powers of conscious deliberation has the familiar ring of something near to the truth. All of us who use computers regularly are aware of their mesmerizing and seductive allure. Although few accept the "reality" presented on the computer screen as a convincing substitute for the real, everyone must acknowledge that, at times, this cyber-world can become a black hole for our time, our consciousness, our lives, perhaps even our souls. In this regard, it takes no great leap of the imagination to relate to the notion that one might be capable of "jacking in" to a virtual world in which we are blinded to reality and stripped of our selfhood.

As a master of imagery, simulation, and illusion, our modern consumer culture salivates over such a prospect, conjuring visions of an electronic feast to be held in a gleaming, virtual, global shopping mall dripping with tantalizing delicacies, inducements, seductions, and entertainments unknown outside of cyberspace. To the culture of the commodity, the vastness of cyberspace surely appears as the ultimate arena in the battle to control consumer consciousness and to manipulate consumer desire. Indeed

---

[123] Baudrillard, *Perfect Crime*, 25.
[124] Baudrillard, *Intelligence of Evil*, 27.
[125] Baudrillard, *Perfect Crime*, 29, 40.

today, in cyberspace, on the Internet, and inside virtual reality, consumer culture is at work constructing powerful domains of global domination, virtual capitalism, and all manner of cyber-financial, techno-promotional manipulations that are like the ones it first built for television back in the early 1960s.

However, beyond the screen, the cyber world is nothing like the world of television. On TV, centralized nodes distribute selected messages to a mass audience of isolated individual viewers who are unable to respond. In cyberspace, all communications are individually directed, free-floating, nonhierarchical, potentially communal, and for the most part, reciprocal.[126] While television assaults us with predigested, shared visions that we are unable to direct and begets shared mass perceptions to which we are unable to respond, the virtual world supplies individuals with the ability to directly acquire virtually any kind of data, make contact with others, participate in virtual communities, and distribute information to a broad public. Watching TV, many of us experience a strange sense of alienation and captivity as though we might be dreaming "someone else's nightmares."[127] In the world of television, we are silent slaves to consumer culture and to the attending media; in cyberspace, we are the media.

The differences between TV and the cyber world of electronic communication is so great that some have predicted that computer connectivity spells the end of consumer culture's pervasive domination. The argument goes that in the cyber world we are no longer slaves to things, that in cyberspace, commodities have been replaced by information, data, and knowledge and an interactive system in which we can all choose, modify, and stabilize, negotiate meanings, as well as recognize, debate, and address other individuals and groups. Further the theory goes that this interconnected cyber world is not without conflict. It is populated by all kinds of people including those whose intent is suspect. In cyberspace we find diversity, complexity, and even cruelty, just like we do in the real world. The presence of diversity and complexity and the resulting confrontations, conflicts, and contradictions are, according to many thinkers, the stuff of reality and thus of freedom from consumer culture. However, the question remains, is this cyber world really a path to freedom or is it just a better, more complete simulation than the one provided by film and television? Or could it be both?

---

[126] Pierre Lévy, *Cyberculture* (Minneapolis and London, University of Minnesota Press, 2001, 205-6.
[127] Lévy, *Cyberculture*, 206.

Consumer Culture in the Age of Information

Regardless of whether this boundless new cyber world leads us to freedom or further ensnares us in consumer culture's web of commodification and illusion, everyone by now recognizes the potential power of this vast web of information, control, and connectivity. Many of those who ponder these things suggest that we have entered a new paradigm, an age in which the basic economic resource is no longer capital, nor natural resources, nor labor, but information and knowledge. In economic terms this line of thought suggest that the primary engines of classical economics, the central wealth-creating activities that allocate capital and resources to the productive uses of labor, have become "productivity" and "innovation," both applications of knowledge to work.[128] In this new paradigm of the so-called Information Age, the emphasis shifts from the material to the immaterial, from physical goods and equipment to know-how and creativity, from real property to intellectual property, from manufacturing to the creation, storage and dissemination of information.

In the logic of modern consumer culture, the cyber world represents nothing more than the latest expansion of the marketplace, and information becomes just another commodity to be packaged and sold. And yet, the marketplace of information is fundamentally different from the physical marketplace. Information has unique properties: it can be at once sold and at the same time retained. Further, raw information—raw data as cyber-speak would term it—is useless unless processed and interpreted. Information is neither knowledge nor wisdom until it is placed in context and acted upon by humans. Still further, and perhaps most importantly, the cyber-world that constitutes the information marketplace is by no stretch of the imagination under the complete control of modern consumer culture, or of anyone or anything else for that matter. Unlike the other media and the spectacular showplaces that populate the physical world of the commodity, the cyber world is so vast, so diverse, so arbitrary, so fluid, that so far, it has been able to resists comprehensive manipulations. Totalitarian governments have tried, but this kind of regulation appears to be far from complete. Governments and multimedia industries follow the cyber-culture as best they can, vainly · attempting to slam on the brakes and slow down what they perceive to be the anarchy of the Internet, but new anarchies appear faster than the old can be shut down.[129]

---

[128] Richard A Lanham, *The Economics of Attention: Style and Substance in the Age of Information* (Chicago and London: The University of Chicago Press, 2006), 4.

[129] Lanham, Economics of Attention, 209.

Although such oppressive bureaucratic attempts to regulate and restrict the cyber world seem doomed to failure, consumer culture remains unconcerned, for it does not seek this kind of control. Its methods are much more subtle. As the culture of the commodity works within this virtual world of digital interconnectivity, it does not seek to restrict our access, nor does it seek to silence all resistance. It allows for resistance, and then attempts to stylize our descent and commodify it. Consumer culture knows that radical cultural and revolutionary social movements cannot be separated or purged from the economy and the marketplace, but they can be appropriated, atomized, diffused, and merged into the system.

Indeed, in a very real way our consumer culture helped to create the Internet in the first place. As most of us know, the Internet was the brainchild of the United States military. It was first developed to enable labs across the county to access supercomputers at a handful of locations. Out of this powerful machine, researchers and students created a vast non-hierarchal public space for the exchange of information, but the public was not fully aware to this cooperative and spontaneous digital system until the end of the 1980s when it became the focus of our consumer culture. In the closing decades of the last century, techno-entrepreneurs began a fight to sell access, organize structure, pillage content, and transform the Internet into a spectacular new space for advertising and promotion.[130]

Predictably, a seemingly endless parade of new social movements and radical activism accompanied the web's commercial success. Although many users espoused programs hostile to the smooth workings of consumer culture, they also presented this culture with opportunities to create new products, make new sales arguments, and channel resistive energies in directions that defuse their power, blend into the fabric of the culture, and become exploitable, even fashionable trends. Consumer culture does not seek to annihilate resistance; it seeks to channel it, to use it, to appropriate its energy and appeal in an endless quest to achieve economic growth and to turn everything into a commodity. The irony is that "Save the Whales" and "You've Come a Long Way, Baby" T-shirts trivialize, institutionalize, commodify, and obscure the true nature of the revolutionary messages that they were originally intended to convey.

In this kind of manipulation, modern consumer culture works its paradoxical power to both free us and dominate us at the same time. The vast, interconnected world of computer-based communications supplies us with the clearest, most compelling insights into the inner working of this culture that we have yet to encounter. In the infinitely complex cyber

---

[130] Lanham, *Economics of Attention*, 208-9.

world, a battle rages. At stake is our freedom to act collectively for the common good. The unique, new paths to community and resistance found in the virtual world supply us with the connectivity we need to break the monomaniacal domination of consumer culture. At the same time, this culture of the commodity uses the new electronic medium to further stupefy us, absorbing, commodifying, and assimilating all efforts to stem its self-perpetuating power. The new electronic age condemns us to an even more spectacular world of illusion, while paradoxically it simultaneously presents us with new possibilities for unfettered communication, coalition, and power.

Chapter Six: Celebrity and Consumer Culture

Celebrity, Individuality, and the Changing Face of Fame

The rise of celebrity culture in America has paralleled the rise of consumer culture, and our absorption in the lives of the famous has evolved as our national values have migrated from a work ethic to an ethic of leisure, consumption, and entertainment. As agents of the consumer culture, modern celebrities offer living proof that these new values hold the key to success and self-realization.

Historically, we have always endowed fame with special meaning. Before the appearance of today's modern consumer culture, we generally regarded our heroes and famous men as gifted individuals pursuing the "highest ends, unfettered by the desire for personal glory." Heroic deeds were thought to be historically validated, and great men and women were elevated to the status of "celebrity" on the wings of their achievement, genius, power, or humanitarian sensitivity. In the age when the American work ethic was ascendant, the national narrative of individual greatness generally outlined a "democratic myth of humble beginnings followed by hard work," success, and fame. With the arrival of twentieth century mass society, the American notion of fame and celebrity began to change. Moving beyond the urban commodity spectacles and gleaming entertainments staged by the infant consumer culture, early films, radio broadcasts, and popular music began to project new images of individual possibility—new discourses that centered on a heightened sense of intimacy with modern celebrities and on anyone's potential access to stardom. In these largely media-driven discourses, America created a new and more accessible hero, broadened the celebrity selection process, and bestowed new kinds of meaning on its public individuals—meanings that corresponded to new, highly accessible forms of consumption.[131]

As America fashioned her new national vision of "stardom," she created a new industry aimed at the reproduction of this vision and at the perpetuation of the notion that anyone could achieve fame and fortune. At its core, the so-called culture industry celebrated the rise of the commodity with new, larger-than-life, infinitely reproducible public personalities. As minions of a depthless popular culture, today's so-called stars are part of a system of false promise, which "offers the reward of stardom only to a random few in order to perpetuate the myth of potential universal success." The notion that almost anyone could be a celebrity helps to placate the masses, to blunt the banality of everyday existence, and to insure the widespread acceptance of the modern condition.[132]

As the heroes of old were replaced by the stars of the twentieth century, the belief that individual success was a product of hard work withered and was supplanted by visions of a new, more arbitrary kind of success born primarily of good luck and favorable circumstance—visions not of discipline and labor but of relaxation and play. The heroes of this new era were to be "idols of consumption" and leisure, not "idols of production" and virtuous toil. These new idols made manifest the promise that the entire social system would be open to "moments of luck"; they offered hope for everyone's success; and thus, they reinforced the status quo.[133] Gone were the traditional heroic markers of genius, achievement, power, and service to the public good. In their place, modern consumer culture created vapid, interchangeable, consumable, public figures that skyrocketed to stardom and celebrity propelled by little more than their widespread visibility. America had shifted her celebrity faith from the old ideology of "achievement-based fame" to the current notion of "media-driven renown."[134]

Moreover, the credentials of our public figures were not the only thing that had changed. The relationship between the powerful and the powerless, the known and the unknown, was also shifting. As the 1970s and 80s unfolded, the American public seized upon new values and a new ethic of leisure and consumption as its media-henchmen fashioned new landscapes of contemporary celebrity. No longer separated from our heroes by barriers of privilege and circumstance, we are today invited to identify

[131] P. David Marshall, *Celebrity and Power: Fame in Contemporary Culture* (Minneapolis: University of Minnesota Press, 1997), 7-9.

[132] Marshall, *Celebrity and Power*, 9-10.

[133] Leo Lowenthal, "The Triumph of Mass Idols," (1944) in *Literature, Popular Culture and Society*, (Palo Alto, Ca: Pacific, 1961), 109-40.

[134] Ellis Cashmore, *Celebrity/Culture* (New York: Routledge, 2006), 7.

with our celebrities. The modern media perpetuates a fantasy of newfound celebrity familiarity in the ever-expanding illusion of "intimacy with distant others."[135] In this intensified atmosphere, we often feel that we actually know our celebrities. We internalize them, identify with them, make them part of our consciousness, part of our lives, just as we do with closest friends.[136] Today our heroes seem to walk among us. Willingly or unwillingly, they surrender themselves to our inspection. With our newfound intimacy, we become ravenous for insider information about celebrities—for details about their romantic lives, for label-by-label breakdowns of the clothes they wear, or for lists of the bars that they frequent.[137] In a close-knit, media-saturated atmosphere of intimate image and life-like spectacle, we attach exaggerated value to information about the private lives of public figures despite the fact that they are often unworthy of our attention. We obsess over these new glossy public personalities, even though many have become celebrities merely by basking in whatever notoriety the media has seen fit to bestow upon them. In the wake of this somewhat random selection process, our emerging consumer culture makes it abundantly clear that it arbitrarily elevates ordinary people to star status. It then becomes equally clear to all that anyone might become a star. In this notion, as in the promise of a lottery, we are lifted out of the drudgery of modern life by the reinforced "conception that there are no barriers in contemporary culture that the individual cannot overcome."[138]

Our current fascination with the world of celebrity resonates with our changing conceptions of individualism. As the modern age appeared, the frontier disappeared, and urbanization and industrialization replaced an agrarian world, Americans found it increasingly difficult to express the cherished American brand of individualism that had evolved from the nation's unique faith in liberty, work, self-sufficiency, property, and the unfettered pursuit of self-interest. In the face of mass society's numbing, conformist regimen, American individualism was on the verge of foundering, and the national ideology of individual distinction and self-reliance was in dire need of shoring up. As the last half of the twentieth century unfolded, the rise of consumer culture and the accompanying widespread fascinations with celebrity attempted to accomplish the ideological shift needed to rescue individualism from the depths of a sea of conformity and right the ship of

[135] John Thompson, *The Media and Modernity: A Social Theory of the Media* (Cambridge: Polity, 1995), 220.

[136] Richard Schickel, *Intimate Strangers: The Culture of Celebrity* (Garden City, NJ: Doubleday and Company, Inc., 1985), 4.

[137] Cashmore, *Celebrity/Culture*, 1.

[138] Marshall, *Celebrity and Power*, 246.

the American individual. Like the old individualism of the frontier, this new brand of American individualism was centered in notions of personal liberty. However, this was no longer just the freedom to work, achieve, and exploit; it now included the freedom to choose what one consumes, including the commodified celebrities the nation had come to adulate. In all of this, the individual still struggles to stand erect at the center of capitalist culture, creating distinctive lifestyles and self-representations out of the meanings contained in the products he or she buys and the celebrities with whom he or she identifies. The economic independence of the "star" operates as a symbol of American freedom and bolsters the original American ideology of the intrinsic, self-correcting goodness accomplished by the free pursuit of one's self-interest. The result is perfect for the advance of modern consumer culture. Since the commodity and the celebrity "express a form of valorization of the individual...that is coherent with capitalism and the associated consumer culture," they serve the system's primary objective: seamless reproduction and growth. [139]

All the while, consumer culture recites its monomaniacal mantra: turning everything and everyone it touches into commodities to be bought and sold in the marketplace. As consumers, we are encouraged to declare our worth by spending money on items that will help us look like, play like, and be like the celebrities with whom we have come to identify. These stars carry special meaning for us, meanings of wealth, beauty, success, toughness, suavity, and so on. They perform endless stimulations, relentlessly teasing us to make ourselves more like them by buying the products they create, endorse, and use.[140] Thus, the modern celebrity is central to consumer culture's ongoing deception in which material goods become constituent parts of a good life, a life "conceived as endless novelty, change, and excitement, as a titillation of the senses by every available stimulant." However, it is not just television, movies and CDs and all of the products created, used, and endorsed by the new media-generated celebrities that are at issue; in a marketplace "obsessed with youth, glamour, sex, money, violence, and celebrity," the new celebrities themselves are converted into products for sale.[141] The intensity of our gaze transforms celebrities into commodities to be marketed, sold, consumed, and used up with a rapidity unimagined by the heroes of old. Indeed, once our voyeurism passes a certain pitch, we are only satisfied by something new, and so we find ourselves continually casting our celebrity heroes into

---

[139] Marshall, *Celebrity and Power*, 17-19.

[140] Cashmore, *Celebrity/Culture*, 15.

[141] Christopher Lasch, *The True and Only Heaven: Progress and Its Critics* (New York: W. W. Norton, 1991), 520.

oblivion and replacing them with prefect clones selected from the countless replicas that are endlessly mass-produced in the consumer culture.[142]

Celebrities and Consumers: Critical Readings

In a glittering world of image, spectacle, simulation, and reproduction celebrities, like everything else, are filled with symbolic meaning. Today's celebrities carry messages that are branded on their public personas by the roles they have assumed on television, in movies, or through military, political, athletic, or other highly visible careers. These messages are indelibly infused into the celebrity's evolving image by intense and repeated performances on a public stage. Part of the alchemy of consumer culture is that it can transfer the meaning carried by celebrities into the products they use and sponsor. This is generally accomplished through celebrity endorsement and advertising. Then, in a second miracle of transformation, these meanings are passed on to the consumers who buy these products. Consumers are constantly rummaging for goods with usable meanings—meanings that can be employed to bolster certain aspects of the self and to hold an uncertain world at bay. For celebrity-meanings to be transferred from endorsed products to consumers, consumers must actively claim these meanings, work with them, and make them their own.[143] Once a consumer successfully incorporates the original celebrity-meaning of an endorsed product into his or her self-image, the process is complete. Modern consumer culture has accomplished another of its invisible transformations: first passing the meaning embodied in the acts and roles of celebrities to the celebrities themselves, then to the products they endorse, and finally to the consumers who purchase these products and use them to modify and enhance their perceived identities. As Grant McCracken puts it:

> Celebrities...are exemplary figures because they are seen to have created the clear, coherent, and powerful selves that everyone seeks. They are compelling partners to the meaning-transfer process because they demonstrate so vividly the process by which these meanings can be assembled and some of the novel shapes into which they can be assembled.[144]

In the shadow of the seemingly weightless and purely symbolic materialistic preoccupations that arise from our vapid obsessions with the

---

[142] Jill Neimark, "The Culture of Celebrity," in *Psychology Today*, May/June, 1995, 56; Elizabeth Bronfen, "Celebrating Catastrophe," in *Angelaki: Journal of Theoretical Humanities*, Vol. 7, No. 2, 181.
[143] McCracken, *Consumer Culture II*, 105-11.
[144] McCracken, *Consumer Culture II*, 112.

lives of the famous, many critics have declared consumer culture to be the domain of the Philistine. Many see the current celebrity culture as a grand illusion that effectively cloaks an American cultural wasteland whose inhabitants are lost in their own depthless, trivial fixations and blind to the impending bankruptcy of the national repository of artistic sensitivity, moral substance, and individual worth. These are the same critics who insist that today's consumer culture, with its far-reaching apparatus aimed at the production and consumption of images, commodities, and staged events, seeks to accomplish the pacification and de-politicalization of the American public.[145] At their most radical, such critics agree with Guy DeBord, who described a so-called "society of the spectacle" in which the forces of an entrenched bureaucratic system wage a "permanent opium war, which stupefies social subjects and distracts them from the most urgent task of real life—recovering the full range of human powers through creative practice."[146]

The stupefaction of the American public by the spectacles of consumer culture and by its countless agents, and especially by the media and advertising, is a well-worn theme. The glamorous celebrities who populate this seemingly depthless culture are part of the current over-simplified landscape of American media, an addicting, proliferating, largely visual panorama that is constantly simplifying its content and familiarizing its heroes by presenting them in blunt, uncomplicated messages that are instantly comprehensible. These critics insist that this crudely commercial media world filled with one-dimensional characters that we immediately recognize and understand, "subsumes, masks, and ultimately destroys" our capacity for subtler, more reflective, and therefore more dangerous confrontations with complex issues. These critics complain that we are presented with seemingly concrete, one-dimensional, close-enough-to-touch heroes who offer us unambiguous symbols requiring nothing of our imagination. The result is what Richard Schickel calls the "new tyranny" of today's celebrity and media culture. Schickel puts forward a damning case charging that such rudimentary messages have left us unable to "imagine in the traditional sense of the word," and incapable of comprehending abstract concepts.

> [We] cannot, it would seem, fill in the blanks that literate culture has traditionally asked its audience to conjure up out of its own memory and experience when it is presented with fictions that have as their purpose the illumination of some truth more curious than the entirely documentary, some subtlety that does not lie entirely in what

---

[145] King, *Spectacle of the Real*, 25.
[146] Debord, *Society of the Spectacle*, Thesis Number 44.

is said, but in the manner of its saying. From this simplification, other simplifications follow. We are the prisoners now of crude—if, in the case of the celebrity lives we so eagerly attend, lingeringly serialized— narrative. It had better be fast moving, action-packed, suspenseful, and full of instantly apprehensible sensation. Above all, it must be peopled with characters we understand as quickly as we understand the full meaning of a nice frosty bottle of Coke....[147]

Although the world around us grows more perplexing, more complex by the minute, we continue to resist attempts to answer complexity with complexity. We continue to insist on clear, simple answers: the news in thirty minutes, the dismissive half-truths contained in catchy sound bites, solutions to the complex problems of self-image and personal acceptance resolved in a new pair of shoes or a trendy car. We want the confidence, beauty, and *savoir faire* that seem to flow from celebrity and the products that celebrities recommend, and yet we seem unaware that our media and our celebrities fail to offer us any depth, that they simply bombard us with a massive barrage of unconnected simplified information delivered without critical or historical perspective. In the face of this unconnected overflow, we can't quite grasp the reality that the result of too much information is to level everything out, to numb our intellect, and to leave us largely clueless. In the face of this onslaught, we blindly allow ourselves to be consoled by a media-driven fantasy. Armed with little more than vague over-simplifications, we maintain the illusion that we are knowledgeable and that we are connected to the world around us in very simple, straightforward ways. Somehow, we unconsciously sense the terrifying possibility that, were we given better information, we would avoid seriously considering the daunting reality that events are beyond our control, beyond the control of any individual, and that "incoherence and even anarchy are loose upon the world."[148] Ignoring any lingering, back-of-the-mind terror, we immerse ourselves in the glittering fantasy world constructed by consumer culture, a vast and enticing landscape of spectacle, image, fashion, and celebrity.

The Breadth of the Celebrity World

Our seemingly insatiable national lust to penetrate the world of the rich and famous and to possess the assorted meanings found there extends to a broad range of celebrity domains. America's fascinated gaze is fixed not only on movie and TV stars, but also on athletes, politicians, musicians, academics, soldiers, businessmen and women, models, artists, writers,

---

[147] Schickel, *Intimate Strangers*, 289-90.
[148] Schickel, *Intimate Strangers*, 291-2.

millionaires, aristocrats, even scoundrels, criminals and murderers. In the voyeuristic world of the famous, the most important mark of distinction is fame itself. Although many of the celebrities we adore do possess talent, charisma, charm, strength, power, or other laudable attributes, at the bottom of it all, the defining characteristic of the celebrity is that he or she is well known. Given the capricious whim of the media and the wandering nature of the public eye, this may appear to be an arbitrary standard, however, it serves us well, for it allows us to sustain the illusion that we can all become stars. If the selection process is arbitrary enough, the turnover large enough, and the field of endeavor broad enough, then the obvious inference is that any one of us might one day be selected.

As we have noted, the turnover is indeed large because we tend to consume our celebrities and cast them off like the disposable products they have become. However, this is not always the case. To reinforce and sustain its penchant for nostalgia, consumer culture elevates certain celebrities to a kind of perpetual "hall of fame." Although some of this kind of permanent enshrinement is the product of the celebrity's individual merit, some is related to prevalent notions of "camp," and "kitsch," those odd, even frivolous, cultural sensibilities in which seemingly passé people and things are re-configured to create new and stylish objects. The enduring legacy of "camp" arises out of a playful kind of attention born of an ironic and often humorously outdated sense of style. Camp celebrates the inevitable failure of style through a complex process. That which was once fantastic becomes timeworn and banal and then later, in the ironic embrace of camp, becomes fantastic again, owing, at least in part, to its former banality. In the odd illumination of camp what is old becomes new again, and moreover what appears very square becomes oddly hip. Like old Flash Gordon comics and B movies, Steve Reeves, Jayne Mansfield, Gina Lollobrigida, Victor Mature, and Bette Davis[149] live on as endearing celebrity exaggerations of styles that long ago became passé.

With their cultural power and substantial personal wealth, today's celebrities appear to the public as symbols of freedom. Although the stars of movies and television are perhaps the most visible and certainly the most obvious examples of the independence of today's celebrity idols, we find this kind of celebrity in many other fields as well. For example, the stars of the popular music scene occupy a well-lit corner of our consumer culture. These celebrities fashion uniquely robust bonds of identity with their adoring audiences and fans. Following the advent of modern recording technology, the popular music industry has mushroomed, and it reached a turning point

---

[149] Sontag, "Notes on Camp."

in the late 1950s and early 60s when the new idiom of "rock" was born. Rock's influence quickly spread laterally to other genres throughout the music world, while at the same time it drew on the rich musical traditions of many other culturally ingrained idioms including blues, country, folk, and bebop. At the center of this new idiom was the "rock star," the rising voice of a growing and increasingly rebellious youth culture. As modern consumer culture reconfigured the social world around consumption and the creation of segmented social identities and leisure-oriented lifestyles, the rock star came to represent a new collective youth identity obsessed with new ethics of sexuality, entertainment, and pleasure. Rock stars stood at the hub of this generational movement eschewing traditional values and (despite their attending reformist rhetoric) often reveling in rebellious decadence, excess, and pleasure without any seeming connection to morality. Although the youth rebellion of the 1960s and early 70s has since been diffused and commodified into a mere stylistic differentiation to be bought and sold in the marketplace, rock stars have maintained their place as symbols of a new, youthful, devil-may-care hedonism. As cultural markers, they express their freedom in their "musical roots, style of dress, manner of speech, and in public displays of sexuality." Through outrageous public behavior, spectacular concerts, and poignant original material, today's "singer-songwriters" appear to control their own destinies. The appearance of such freedom draws audiences to these musical heroes creating an authentic and intimate bond between celebrity and fan that is often stronger and more lasting bonds than those found in other celebrity domains. [150]

The world of sport produces similar robust fan/celebrity bonds. Certainly, it is clear to all observers that, since America's consumer culture reached maturity back in the last third of the twentieth century, the prominence of sport in the popular culture has skyrocketed, and most people would be quick to conclude that our growing passion for athletic events is a product of the growth and power of television. Indeed, the intensity, action, and pageantry of modern sporting events, overflowing with color and crowds and competition, provide perfect settings for the popular culture to create spectacles of heroic proportion. Offering live, spontaneous action, sporting events serve as ideal subjects for television's older documentary style, while at the same time, they have facilitated the development of the medium's recent transformation from documentary messenger to purveyor of astonishing imagery, fantasy, illusion, and hyperbolic spectacle. Sporting events are today hyped on TV in pervasive and seemingly endless rituals of words and images. Games are analyzed, replayed, and broken down in

---

[150] Marshall, *Celebrity and Power*, 161.

every aspect of strategy, athleticism, and competitive drive. Played and replayed in stop-action, slow-motion, zoom-in precision, today's sporting events are accompanied by fantastic graphics, uplifting music, and over-the-top commentary creating frenzies of excitement in even the most lopsided mismatches. Clearly, television has changed sport forever; it has transformed simple games into spectacles of the unreal.

However, television is both message and messenger, both the instrument of change and the reporter of the news of the changes it begets. In the case of sport, the news is not the increasing popularity and expanding technology of televised athletic spectacles but rather the radical change in our most fundamental perceptions of sport. In the former age of the capitalist ethic, the sporting focus was on competition, on the game, the standings, the contest, the team. In today's consumerist age, the focus has shifted. It is no longer centers on the team, or even on the game, but rather on the individual sports stars and their blinding celebrity.

In the era when the work ethic was ascendant, the stars of sport stood as powerful symbols for the rewards of hard work, as well as for fair play and sportsmanship. Today, like almost all celebrities, the sports celebrity stands as a symbol of individual freedom garnered somewhat capriciously and exercised through wealth and power. Although most of us recognize that our heroes of the diamond, gridiron, and hardwood achieved fame through both natural ability and hard work, many of our poorest citizens bond to the sports celebrity as living proof that in America the downtrodden can still rise to spectacular heights. Most of us will admit that the well-worn American myth of lofty rewards possible within the capitalist work ethic has lost its luster. Today, most realize that no matter how hard one may work, it is virtually impossible for an individual to rise from the underclass to become a captain of industry. At the same time, our notions of fair play have given way to competitions in which more or less anything goes. In the resulting ethical void, Major League Baseball, the NFL, and the NBA are filled with examples of individuals who rose from the depths of poverty to become millionaires and the brightest stars in the celebrity heavens. In its ongoing efforts to subdue the masses by illustrating that anyone might achieve stardom, today's consumer culture has discarded Horatio Alger in favor of Michael Jordan.

Moreover, this culture of the commodity has yet another use for the superstars it creates. As it has progressed from its infancy at the turn of the twentieth century to its ascendancy at the turn of the twenty-first, the forces of the marketplace have overpowered and corrupted the pure world of sport. Games no longer exist for their own sake, but for the purpose of marketing, and the celebrities they create exist not just to hit home runs and score touchdowns, but to create demand for commodities. In a self-replicating pageant of media frenzy, the commercials that sports stars make while exploiting their fame to sell products serve to broaden and enhance the renown of these stars, thus making them even more visible, more popular, that they might make even more effective ads to sell even more products, which, in turn, make them even more visible, and so on. Nike commercials carried the image of Michael Jordan to the entire world, and in this sense it was Nike, and not the Bull's domination of the NBA, that made Jordan a true global superstar[151] and an agent of expanding globalism.[152]

Moving beyond the worlds of entertainment and sport, there are many more domains of modern life that generate celebrities of their own. These include the realms of art, business, literature, and many others. The realm of contemporary politics is notable; celebrities themselves become politicians and politicians regularly enlist the support of celebrities to invigorate their campaigns and endear themselves to voters. Today, controversy envelops the world of the celebrity politician and the celebrity-turned-political activist. This controversy turns on the nature of the voter/politician relationship and on the effect of celebrity and the media on the sacred bond of representation that binds politicians to voters. Critics charge that, since the faithful representation of the popular will is based on clear communications between politician and voter, the introduction of media frenzy, subliminal marketing, and celebrity endorsement can only serve to garble rational communication and corrupt representational bonds. These critics not only insist that the modern media (especially television) substitute political appearance for political substance, but they also point to a process that burdens the modern political campaign with astronomical costs giving rise to all kinds of additional evils.

What these critics are saying with all this lofty rhetoric is that politics has entered the world of the commodity. Nothing escapes the all-encompassing grasp of modern consumer culture, certainly nothing as visible as politics. It reaches out and pulls the political campaign into its glittering worlds of the commodity. Television, spectacle, celebrity, image, and illusion all fill today's candidates with countless new and fluid signs and meanings, thus transforming these candidates, themselves, into commodities to be bought and sold in the marketplace of the election booth. Indeed, "the modern product marketing campaign provides the underlying model for the modern political election campaign," stimulating subtle irrational appeals and

---

[151] Naomi, Klein, *No Logo* (London: Flamingo, 2002), 52.
[152] Cashmore, *Celebrity/Culture*, 236.

hidden meanings aimed at consumers (voters), while outwardly maintaining the appearance of rationality.[153] In today's consumer culture, all candidates are inducted into the popular culture, and all are christened as celebrities, whether or not they come from the world of entertainment or sports, or from the legal profession, the military or business, and whether or not they surround themselves with stars like Kevin Costner, Oprah Winfrey, or Bruce Springsteen.

Beyond the campaign, these political celebrities are imbued with new even more complex bundles of meaning. Once elected, they are seen as cogs in our democratic system, working components that represent the interests of complex constituencies. The perception is that, through the meanings attached to the politician-turned-celebrity, the system can interpret and understand the popular will. However, the processes of government, the political campaign, and the surrounding media circuses fill the commodified political celebrity with myriad other signs, symbols, and meanings as well. As commodities, American politicians radiate spectacles of lofty promise and glittering illusion. Just like products in the mall, they glow with a luster so bright that they are often able to hide the imperfections in the system that gives them life. However, unlike the largely opaque world of the true commodity, in which our consumer culture is effectively able to hide broad societal imperfections from the consumer's view, today's politicians, despite their commodity status, remain somewhat translucent. Assisted by the media, a wisely constructed American political system still operates with a degree of transparency, thus allowing us glimpses of flaws, transgression, and abuses that often stimulate at least some level of resistance, but more often stimulate only cynicism.

In answer to charges of the blurring of American political rhetoric in the age of the commodity, one can only say that political representation is itself "a cultural act, which seeks to realize a form of political attractiveness through the gestures and images of popular culture."[154] Perhaps the manipulation of the consumer culture signals the demise of representative politics. More likely, it is just an added dimension to the old political and representational imagery, an affirmation of the highly symbolic character of American life and the American political process.

Finally, any assessment of the present American obsession with celebrity would be incomplete without a discussion of our current fascination with criminals, sociopaths, and villains of all sorts. To be sure, a certain prurient

[153] Marshall, *Celebrity and Power*, 205.
[154] John Street, "Celebrity Politicians: Popular Culture and Political Representation," in *The British Journal of Politics and International Relations*, 2004 Vol. 6, 449.

interest in crime, corruption, and the dark and seamy underworlds of modern life flows from nothing more perverse than a natural quirk of human nature. Nonetheless, our current fascination with the most notorious denizens of these realms has clearly reached alarmingly unnatural levels. In American popular culture, the standard for celebrity becomes fame itself without necessary attachment to any value judgments, and thus, famous criminals often become celebrities. Today, we experience self-perpetuating cycles of public absorption in morbid crimes and those who commit them, which in turn drive media-hype, which in turn drives even more heightened public absorption. In a world where fame is celebrated for its own sake, the relationship between fame and infamy quickly becomes distorted; the infamous become famous, and the word "infamy" passes from the language.

Certainly, Americans have always tended to make heroes of certain outlaws. Jesse James, Billy the Kid, Bonnie and Clyde, and Pretty Boy Floyd all come immediately to mind. However, a careful examination of such legendary lawbreakers reveals that these criminals stood upon the heroic pedestal of public adulation owning to a widespread (although often unconscious) perception that their crimes symbolized a kind of extra-legal justice. Such a notion is fraught with political overtones. In the public mind, it placed the offender in the role of rebel rather than that of criminal. Inherent in such a Robinhood-like perception was a public dissatisfaction with the social system, with the justice doled out by the established legal system, and widespread notions of individual powerlessness.[155] The enduring legends of these hero-criminals focused on the rebellion represented by their crimes and tended to ignore the bloody details and immediate circumstances of many brutal and unspeakable deeds.

Today's celebrity criminals are rarely of this sort. Like all symbols in American consumer culture, the symbolism attached to contemporary celebrity-criminals is far more complex, blurred, mixed, and fluid. Nonetheless, our current fascination clearly extends to the details and circumstances of their crimes, the bloodier and more perverse the better, and, as with all our celebrities, we hunger for details regarding the private lives of notorious perpetrators. Although they may not exactly be heroes, they *are* well known, and in popular culture this alone generally elevates one to celebrity status.

---

[155] Paul Kooistra, "Criminals as Heroes: Linking Symbol to Structure," in *Caliber: Journals of the University of California Press*, 1990, Vol. 13, No. 2, 217–239.

Celebrity and Hyper-reality

In the final analysis, almost everything we can say about the grand illusions and abundant meanings and signs that characterize our depthless commodity culture, we can also say about the current culture of celebrity. In our discussions of American consumer culture, we have used adjectives like "intensified," "dream-like," "stimulating," superficial," "illusory," "artificial," "intoxicating," "banal," and "simulated"; likewise we have employed nouns like "spectacle," "fantasy-world," "identification," "manipulation," and "fascination." All of these can be accurately used to describe our current preoccupation with the world of celebrity.

For example, in our discussions of the radical theories of the French post modernist Jean Baudrillard, we have touched on the notion of the "hyper-reality" that commodity culture imposes on our everyday lives, intensifying, distilling, replacing, and finally excluding the enervations of the reality upon which it was once based.[156] For Baudrillard, hyper-reality is the product of an overproduction of signs, a saturation of free-floating symbols and allusions flowing from generations of simulations that ultimately produce "models of a real without origin or reality,"[157] copies of copies for which there is not original. According to Baudrillard, the symbols and simulations of the hyper-real are attached to virtually everything we experience, and their meanings are in constant flux depending on context, interaction, circumstance, and myriad other situational variables. In a world where everything is a commodity, all products are impregnated with countless meandering symbols signifying romance, exotica, desire, beauty, fulfillment, progress, savvy, and so on, depending on the circumstance. The result, according to Baudrillard, is a total "aestheticization" of the real and the eventual loss of any stable meaning.[158] As radical as all this may sound, if we place our present celebrity culture under a microscope, we will quickly discover examples that offer compelling evidence that Baudrillard is right. For example, one description of hyper-reality postulates that it is "a public space of contained and intensified representation, a stimulating but safe spectacle which excludes while it distills the enervations of the reality upon which it is modeled."[159] A close examination of celebrity culture will reveal that it is indeed a "public space," which is clearly "contained" and yet, at the same time, it most certainly offers us "intensified" and often "spectacular representations" that are both "stimulating and safe." Most importantly, the world of celebrity tends to

---

[156] Slater, "Going Shopping," 198.
[157] Baudrillard, "Simulacra and Simulations," 166.
[158] Featherstone, *Consumer Culture and Postmodernism*, 68.
[159] Slater, "Going Shopping," 198.

close out the real world upon which it is built, and replace it with "distilled, intensified, and increasingly fantastic representations." We need only pick up any tabloid "movie" magazine to confirm all of this.

In *Simulations*, Baudrillard himself alludes to the hyper-real's association with celebrity. In describing a world in which the real and the imaginary are confused and aesthetic fascination is everywhere, he tells us that "a kind of non-intentional, parody hovers over everything, of technical simulating, of indefinable fame to which is attached an aesthetic pleasure."[160] Here Baudrillard is suggesting that consumer culture attempts to turn everything, even fame itself, into a work of art, thus completely destroying the distinction between high art, popular art, and everyday life, and, in so doing, creating an "aesthetic hallucination of reality."[161] Again, this may seem radical, and yet closer examination of the current celebrity culture reveals a certain truth in this point of view. As we shall see, consumer culture creates a kind of "token art," in which everything, even the banal, becomes aesthetic. We find this all around us: in advertising, in spectacular displays of glitter and glitz, in notions of "camp" and "funk," in our changing concepts of fashion and style, even in the glamour and allure of celebrity. Indeed, in many ways, we attempt to create "celebrity-works-of-art" through our fascinations with the lives of the rich and famous. At the same time, we recognize a certain playful "parody" in such "simulations." In the end, we are both amused and fascinated by all of consumer culture's tabloid manipulations, and we succumb to a celebrity world in which the real and the simulated have become so confused that simulations have become real, just as they have in the worlds of consumption, art, and in the popular culture in general.

So it is that the human commodities of the celebrity world illustrate the ability of all commodities to take up a wide range of imagistic and symbolic associations, which overlay their utility creating an endless series of simulations that constantly interact and "play off each other."[162] For Jean Baudrillard, it is this endless piling up these signs and simulations that creates the present hyper-reality, an unstable, often playful world of artificial stimulation, symbolic illusion, and fluidity of meaning—a world in which everything has become aesthetic.

---

[160] Baudrillard, *Simulations*, 151.
[161] Baudrillard, *Simulations*, 148.
[162] Featherstone, *Consumer Culture and Postmodernism*, 99.

CHAPTER SEVEN: CONSUMER CULTURE AND EVERYDAY LIFE

The Aesthetic of the Everyday

Jean Baudrillard's notion of the world as an "aesthetic hallucination" may at first appear both baffling and radical. However, like so much of Baudrillard's work, his ideas regarding hyper-reality and the aestheticization of contemporary life, when tempered with a careful reading, the proper reflection, and perhaps reinforced by an evening of TV or a trip to the mall, offer valuable insights into the current state of affairs in the West. When stripped of hyperbole and decoded, Baudrillard's insights illuminate important trends in the way we have come to approach our everyday lives and the world around us. Still, this kind of examination is not always easy. How can art be everywhere?[163] What does Baudrillard mean when he speaks of an all-encompassing "aesthetic hallucination of reality"?[164] Is such an illusion the natural consequence of modern consumer culture's runaway proliferation of symbol, sign, and image?

There are several answers to these questions, and each implies slightly different connotations of the word "aesthetic." In its simplest form, "aesthetic" refers to an appreciation of beauty. More complex definitions of the term extend its meaning to encompass broader matters of taste including notions of what constitutes art. Finally, the contemplation of such lofty sensitivities sometimes lends even subtler dimensions to the term. When we speak of "aestheticism" we not only refer to beauty and art, we may also wish to imply an exaggerated devotion to these (or perhaps to any) metaphysical

---

[163] Baudrillard, *Simulations*, 151.
[164] Baudrillard, *Simulations*, 148.

conceptions—a devotion that sometimes leaves us out of touch with practical matters. Explanations of Baudrillard's sweeping conceptions of the aesthetic hyper-reality that characterizes the world of the commodity rely on all these nuances of meaning and point to forces found both inside and outside of the art world.

First, as we have seen, there are many ways by which modern consumer culture tends to blur the distinction between high art and popular culture. This is nothing new. The process began with the invention of the printing press and has continued throughout the modern age, first with the introduction of photography and film, and later with radio, television, and of course, the internet. The technological ability to reproduce and proliferate images and sounds has the effect of bringing formal art, which once resided only in unique objects or performances, in particular hallowed icons, or in singular cherished moments, down to the popular level where it can be experienced by all and at any time. As Walter Benjamin put it back in 1936, "The cathedral leaves its locale to be received in the studio...the choral production, performed in the auditorium or in the open air, resounds in the drawing room."[165] This endless simulating, mechanical and electronic reproduction of art, in turn, has the effect of removing the "aura" from individual works of art. Once removed from its pedestal and placed amid the teeming masses, art becomes the property of the popular culture, which quickly has its way with the old art, copying, altering, borrowing, debasing, and all the while attaching its own commercial and highly fluid symbolic codes. High art thus disappears, its "critical transcendence" watered down by its mixture with the forms of the popular culture and with the experiences of everyday life.

At the same time, the art world, led by the *avant-garde*, has staged a series of rebellions that seem to be bent on proving that anything, even the most banal of objects or experiences, can be art—not the subject of art, but art itself. Notable among the early movements were Dada and Surrealism with their bold attempts to show that even the most common of everyday objects could be works of art. The "ready-mades" of Marcel Duchamp were typical. Likewise, Pop Art, typified by Andy Warhol's soup cans, later explored similar themes, and along related lines the 1960s saw the beginning of numerous attempts to free art from the yoke of traditional forms and venues. "Happenings," landscape art, and more recently, extravagant multimedia presentations constituted attempts from within the art world to break down

---

[165] Walter Benjamin, "The Work of Art in the Age of Mechanical Reproduction," in *Illuminations* (New York: Harcourt, Brace and World,1968), 219-253.

the barriers separating art from the popular culture and from everyday life.[166] In the process, graphic design, commercial art, and advertising not only became confused with art but they also made their way into the museum. Mike Featherstone puts it nicely:

> Many artists have relinquished their commitment to high culture and *avant-gardism* and have adopted an increasingly open attitude towards consumer culture and now show a willingness to truck with other cultural intermediaries, image-makers, audiences, and publics. Hence, with the parallel purposes of the expansion of the role of art within consumer culture and the deformation of enclaved art with its separate prestige structure and lifestyle, a blurring of *genres* and tendencies has occurred.[167]

As a result of all of this, when a mature consumer culture began to emerge, art was already well on its way to becoming a helpless and debased captive of commodification, promotion, and trade. In creating the spectacles for which it was to become so well known, modern consumer culture further mixed and blended the old art with commercial graphics, television, the internet, and contemporary design. Carefully art-directing virtually everything today, this new culture of the commodity constantly fashions new dream-worlds with carefully cultivated "looks" and attaches myriad signs and symbols to its every creation. All the while, it embosses everything with its own commercial kind of beauty creating a reality that drips with glitz and fashion and flaunts its own highly self-conscious stylistic aesthetic. With an unswerving focus on its own evolving sense of commodified beauty, our consumer culture "impregnates" our current world with a new aesthetic, creating a reality so saturated with likenesses of the real, that, to use Baudrillard's words, it becomes "confused with its own image."[168] Surrounded by a gleaming sea of aesthetic reproductions and simulations so vast and so convincing, we soon lose our way and are unable to distinguish the real from the copy. At this point a ubiquitous new stylized vision of art begins to take hold.

According to Baudrillard, our disorientation upon this sea of simulation is primarily the result of the overproduction of the signs, meanings, and codes that are attached to commodities and to commodity-related reproductions and simulations—an overproduction that leads to saturation, aesthetic fascination, and the loss of any stable meaning.[169] Here we encounter the deeper metaphysical dimension of the aesthetic, a dimension in which the devotion to beauty and art is so focused that it destroys one's grounding

---

[166] Featherstone, *Consumer Culture and Postmodernism*, 66.

[167] Featherstone, *Consumer Culture and Postmodernism*, 25.

[168] Baudrillard, *Simulations*, 151.

[169] Featherstone, *Consumer Culture and Postmodernism*, 15.

in the real-world. For Baudrillard, in the consumer culture's world of endless reproductions, everything—even the everyday, the banal—becomes aesthetic, thus "de-realizing reality"[170] and moving us into the realm of "hyper-reality," which he describes as an "aesthetic hallucination of the real."[171]

Couched in these terms, all this sounds radical indeed, and yet it is easy to see that this kind of aesthetic hallucination is exactly what Charles Baudelaire first saw in the mid-nineteenth century Paris arcades and what Walter Benjamin later found in the writings of Baudelaire. Moreover, this kind of loss of realistic awareness lies at the very heart of Marx's notion of commodity fetishism and is implied in all the various "spins" Marx's ideas have been given not only by the Frankfurt School and by all neo-Marxists ever since, but also by scholars and observers of virtually every color and stripe. Most to the point, Baudrillard's notion of hyper-reality and its myriad aesthetic fabrications are clearly illustrated today almost everywhere—in theme parks, malls, theaters, on TV, as well as on the internet and on every street corner and in every shop. We need only open our eyes to see it gleaming before us on billboards, in architecture, displays, printed advertisements, packages, clothing, hairstyles, makeup, and commodities of all sorts.

Whether we see these ubiquitous everyday aesthetic creations as a hallucination or as reality itself, most of us today buy into its glitzy stylistic allure. Whether we are fascinated, transfixed, and duped by hallucinations or not, we are all drawn to style, fashion, and to gleaming commodities because in them we can find the material to construct new and satisfying individual identities in an otherwise alienating world. As the factories, cities, and bureaucracies of the Modern Age methodically plow under the old building blocks of personal identity and plunder the old individualism, consumer culture comes to our rescue with new freedoms, new symbols, and new possibilities for our battered uniqueness. Using the cultural signs attached to the consumer goods we purchase we can express ourselves and our individuality by exploring new tastes, new sensations, and new realms of distinction within a dynamic social field where the old coordinates are rapidly disappearing.[172] In a sense, the new lifestyles we create using clothes, leisure pastimes, eating and drinking preferences, homes, cars, and myriad new spheres of interest are themselves things of beauty. In this regard, we pick up the torch of aestheticism from popular culture and fashion our own personal aesthetics in the unique lifestyles we create. Thus, completing

---

[170] Wolfgang F. Haug, *Critique of Commodity Aesthetics* (Oxford: Polity Press, 1986), 52.
[171] Baudrillard, *Simulations*, 148.
[172] Featherstone, *Consumer Culture and Postmodernism*, 83.

modern consumer culture's project for the aestheticization of everyday life, we quite literally attempt to turn our everyday lives into works of art.

The notion of turning one's life into a living work of art has a long history. The idea became an important theme in the development of the modern artist countercultures that had their birth in the Parisian *bohème* and *avant-garde* movements of the mid-nineteenth century. Balzac, Baudelaire, Comte d'Orsay and Montesquieu were fascinated with the notion of a life lived as "a pleasing artistic whole" in the "pursuit of new tastes and sensations."[173] Certainly, Baudelaire's *flâneur*, the dandy who makes his body, his behavior, his feelings and passions, his very existence a work of art,"[174] exemplifies these early trends, just as nineteenth-century dandies in general reflect the same project. Notable in this regard was Beau Brummel, who "stressed the quest for a special superiority through the construction of an uncompromising exemplary lifestyle in which an aristocracy of spirit manifested itself in a contempt for the masses and the heroic concern with the achievement of originality and superiority of dress, demeanor, personal habits, and even furnishings."[175] Oscar Wilde recognized the aesthetic component in this tradition when he suggested that the ideal aesthete should "realize himself in many forms," and more recently Richard Rorty has described the good life as "revolving around the desire to enlarge one's self and to explore more and more possibilities."[176] Today there are many who have turned to an aesthetic justification of life, and many more who at least open themselves up to being shaped aesthetically. Following a tradition that goes all the way back to the Romantics, such modern aesthetes seek continuous learning and enrichment, explore new values, and exhibit a curiosity in which the artist and the intellectual are viewed as heroes, and style, the stylization of life, and ever-renewable lifestyle are the central focus.[177]

Modern consumer culture readily facilitates this kind of aesthetic of self-expansion. Today it supplies us with breathtakingly diverse landscapes of choices, which are becoming increasingly difficult to organize or decipher. The range of products, activities, and options available today are perhaps as far from the predicted conformist manipulations of modern mass

---

[173] Featherstone, *Consumer Culture and Postmodernism*, 67.

[174] Michel Foucault, "What is Enlightenment," in Paul Rabinow, ed., *The Foucault Reader* (Harmondsworth, Penguin, 1986), 41-2.

[175] Rosalind H. Williams, *Dream Worlds: Mass Consumption in Late Nineteenth Century France* (Berkley: California University Press, 1982, 107ff, cited in Featherstone, *Consumer Culture and Postmodernism*, 67.

[176] Richard Shusterman, "Postmodern Aestheticism: A New Moral Philosophy?" in *Theory, Culture, Society*, Vol. 5, No. 2, 1988, 337-55, cited in Featherstone, *Consumer Culture and Postmodernism*, 67.

[177] Featherstone, *Consumer Culture and Postmodernism*, 48.

society as can be imagined. Quite the opposite, they seem to represent a vast, "autonomous," and "playful space beyond determination"—a space so vast and diverse that there are those who postulate that this profusion of choice constitutes a significant movement toward "the breakdown of the old hierarchies of fashion, style, and taste in favor of an egalitarian and tolerant acceptance of differences."[178] The notion that our efforts to bolster our waning individual identities by fashioning diverse individual lifestyles and adopting distinct personal aesthetics from images, signs, and symbols attached to an endless array of commodity choices is not new. However, the idea that these attempts to rescue American individualism by rummaging in a hollow consumerism leads us in the direction of universal tolerance and acceptance is revolutionary indeed. Such a notion suggests that consumer culture both frees us and enslaves us at the same time—that it corrupts us with its shallow materialism, while at the same time and perhaps ironically, it lifts us up out of narrow-mindedness, prejudice, and intolerance by championing diversity.

Beyond Individualism

Regardless of whether constructing personal identities using the vast array of commodities and experiences found in today's consumer culture corrupts us or lifts us to new heights of tolerance and diversity, many critics still point to fundamental instabilities inherent in a world where the artificial is so easily confused with the real. Many suggest that the current consumer environment with its dazzling spectacles, unending flow of sign and symbol, and depthless veneer has the effect of moving us "beyond individualism" into new, disjointed, "aesthetic paradigms" involving heightened intensities and "temporary emotional communities."[179] Sociologists speak of "fragmented" or "de-centered" subjects, suggesting that in modern societies the construction of our personal identities through goods is an "inconclusive process, a never-ending endeavor which cannot provide...a stable identity." Although most agree that today's commodity culture provides a maximum of individual specificity, many conclude that identities fabricated through consumption generally prove to be "ambivalent," temporary and "increasingly reflexive pursuits." Such critics insist that, in attempting to turn our lives into works of art by piecing together aesthetically pleasing "lifestyle collages" from goods and experiences, we fail to project "a unitary and coherent self," [180]

---

[178] Featherstone, *Consumer Culture and Postmodernism*, 84.
[179] Michel Maffesoli. "Jeux de Masques: Postmodern Tribalism," in *Design Issues*, Vol. 41, 1-2, 1988, 141-151.
[180] Sassatelli, *Consumer Culture*, 148.

because we are unable to manage such a complex and "highly specific set of different roles." In the end, our ongoing, everyday struggles to adapt, change, and reinvent our teetering commodity-based identities serve only to expand the culture, whose single unswerving goal is simply the growth and perpetuation of the system.

All this notwithstanding, there remains a still deeper critique of the everyday consumer world, an all-encompassing criticism that goes well beyond our quest for our lost individualism. This new postmodern critique suggests that in the wake of new commodity forms, modes of consumption, and intensified market activity, "daily life itself has become more fluid, instantaneous, and immediate, more cosmopolitan and intersected at every juncture by other life-worlds and cultural influences than ever before." Such a critique suggests that the recent destabilization or "de-centering" of the modern self is characterized by a lack of understanding of what it means to be "located as a conscious subject, existing in a particular time within a particular place," and articulated by a stable network of social and cultural relationships. This is the critique of the postmodern, a cultural dominant that is predicated on "the rejection of the notion that objectivity and essential truths and meanings can ever be articulated successfully."[181] In the disappearance of stable social meaning, the postmodern theorizes a "schizophrenic experience of everyday life" characterized by new types of consumption, planned obsolescence, an ever more rapid rhythm of fashion and styling changes, and the penetration of advertising, television, the internet, and the media...throughout society."[182] For the post modernist, consumer culture represents a "radical disruption" of life in which everything becomes an object of consumption and history itself is stripped of its former meaning, continuity, and context. Martyn Lee goes right to the heart of the postmodern aesthetic:

> Previous styles, symbolic codes, cultural movements and artifacts [are] now stripped of their original contexts and meanings... [and] juxtaposed into a bricolage or "pastiche" of retro-chic and nostalgia. Such an aesthetic...invites a fascination, rather than a contemplation, of its contents: it celebrates surfaces and exteriors rather than looking for or claiming to embody (modernist) depth; it foregrounds the materiality of, and the discontinuity between, signifiers while dissolving the hermeneutic possibilities of the signified; it renders the critical distinction between high cultural and the popular culture obsolete; and it erases several of the key cultural boundaries of separation that

---

[181] Lee, *Consumer Culture Reborn*, 141-2.
[182] Frederic Jameson, "Postmodernism and Consumer Society," in H. Foster, ed., *Postmodern Culture* (London: Pluto Press, 1985), 124-5.

have previously existed between discrete cultural forms. In short, the postmodern aesthetic transforms all cultural content into objects for immediate consumption rather than texts of contemplative reception or detached and intellectual interpretation."[183]

Such is the nature of Postmodernism, or what Fredric Jameson was famously called "the cultural logic of late capitalism," and Jean Baudrillard calls hyper-reality. Whether we accept these radical postmodern notions or simply find ourselves staggered by the increasing velocity of change in the modern world, the ironclad logic that today supports the vast array of commodities, spectacles, and illusions manifest in today's consumer culture has become a very real part of our everyday lives. It has altered our social, political, and economic orientations, our systems of belief, our values and norms, as well as our individualism and modes of self-identification. It has transformed us into both the willing slaves and the grateful beneficiaries of a fully automatic system of endless consumption and intensified experience that appears to be beyond the control of anyone—a system that endlessly simulates reality and seeks only its own growth and perpetual reproduction.

---

[183] Lee, *Consumer Culture Reborn*, 143.

CHAPTER EIGHT: THE IDEOLOGY CONSUMER CULTURE

Defining Ideology

To function smoothly and to perpetually reproduce itself, modern consumer culture requires a unique ideological climate hospitable to its operations, manipulations, and growth. Beginning with the growth of capitalism, the rise of the commodity, and the development of the economic, social, and political institutions of the modern era, American consumer culture has produced dramatic shifts in American values, morals, ideals, and beliefs creating an intellectual climate increasingly conducive to its growth. These elemental ideological changes have involved shifting national notions regarding the source of individual identity, the meanings of liberty, emancipation, and progress, as well as the relationship between work and leisure. Today's consumer culture indelibly and invisibly implants its complex self-serving ideological mantra in the American mind in the same way that it promotes and markets vast arrays of commodities.

Many scholarly discussions of ideology take Marx's views as a jumping off place. According to Marx, ideology, like commodity fetishism, is blind to the conditions from which it arises. In the Marxian view, ideology masks the real social relations of production creating an illusionary "false consciousness" and an "upside-down reality," that favor the status quo and support the ruling classes in their exploitation of the under-classes. To use Marxian terms, society's "appearance" is not the same as its "essence." This false "appearance" is not a product of man's inability to make accurate observations, but rather it flows from the very nature of capitalist society itself, which, according to Marx, inherently presents a distorted "appearance."

Thus, in the Marxian view, it is the role of ideology to conceal the "essence" of society and to obscure "the true nature of the commodity as the artificial manipulator of consumer needs and the mask hiding the exploitation of one class by another." [184] For Marx, the commodity is an ideological agent, and in a Marxian world, the ideology of the commodity constitutes a perceived representation that "acts functionally on men via a process that escapes them."[185]

For many today, the Marxian view, with its unflinching focus on class relations, appears a bit too narrow, and modern scholars have migrated to broader notions of "identity politics" embracing a more complex reading of contemporary cultural patterns. Nonetheless, whether or not one is inclined to agree with Marxian theory, Marx's ideas still have their value, and today examples of cynical ideological manipulation can be found seemingly everywhere. Many contemporary critics contend that in America the flag of our sacred national ideology often manipulatively waves in defense all kinds of dubious causes blinding citizens to the abuses of the dominant system. Indeed, many observers contend that the American military-industrial-economic complex maintains its denomination over American society by brandishing patriotic, ideological banners of freedom and nationalistic unity while it rides rough-shod over the very ideas it purports to champion. These critics contend that, at its heart, such ideology seeks to force "the majority, whom it exploits, to define their interests as narrowly as possible."[186] Indeed, we often hear the cynics among us point to ideology as little more than a "calculating conspiracy of false ideas manipulated by the dominant classes."

Today critics of all stripes rail against the constant manipulation of our treasured American ideals. Many characterize the ongoing ideological manipulations as "a set of omissions and gaps rather than lies smoothing over contradictions, appearing to provide answers to questions which in reality they evade, and masquerading as coherence in the interest of social relations generated by and necessary to the reproduction of the existing mode of production."[187] At the extreme, we find the notion of the culture industry, with its vision of "a contemporary society in which everyday culture and social identity" are "manufactured at the whim of big business and the state

[184] David B. Downing and Susan Bazargan, "Image and Ideology: Some Preliminary Histories and Problems," in David B. Browning and Susan Bazargan, ed. *Image and Ideology in Modern/Postmodern Discourse* (Albany, NY: State University Press of New York, 1991), 253.

[185] Louis Althusser, "Ideology and the State," in *Lenin and Philosophy and Other Essays* (London: Verso, 1971), 155, quoted in Lee, *Consumer Culture Reborn*, 44.

[186] John Berger, *Ways of Seeing* (London: BBC/Penguin, 1972), 154, quoted in Lee, *Consumer Culture Reborn*, 19.

[187] Catherine Belsey, *Critical Practice* (London: Methuen, 1980), 57-8, quoted in Lee, *Consumer Culture Reborn*, 43.

apparatus," a notion in which social consciousness itself is produced "almost as effortlessly as the assembly lines produce automobiles or bars of soap."[188]

All this notwithstanding, there are others who suggest that the ongoing American ideology of modern capitalism and the evolving ideology of consumer culture are not complete in their domination—that contradictions and avenues of resistance exist. Central to many of these arguments is the notion that, despite its dominant tendencies, the consumer culture has supplied consumers with new weapons of subversion—that to prefect the consumption ethic, consumer culture has enfranchised consumers with material and symbolic resources of rebellion. The argument goes that the "democratization of consumption and the opportunities made possible by the affluent society" not only open fertile markets, but in so doing, also make available to consumers, and to consumer groups, material and symbolic objects that can serve as "subversive cultural resources." Rock music comes immediately to mind, as do any number of radical youth cults, trends and fads. At another level, the massive expansion of the educational sector (despite its use as a platform for disseminating propaganda for the ideology of the *status quo*) has nonetheless provided a powerful political and social literacy from which new insights into the economic and political system can be gleaned.[189] In this regard, the emerging culture of the commodity may be opening up possibilities for its own interrogation and unleashing the potential means by which the very economic and political ideologies that support the new culture can be placed under scrutiny.[190]

To sidestep this ongoing controversy and for the purposes of examining the ideas and values that support the operations of modern consumer culture, let us employ something of a "neutral" definition of ideology, a definition that includes neither inherent domination nor radical subversion. Let us simply say that ideology is a kind of orientation, a system of beliefs and assumptions that includes values, symbols, ideals, cosmologies, norms, ideas, and modes of self-identification. Let us also say that our ideological view of the world is not static but rather in constant flux, a dynamic product of social practice constantly in the process of reproducing itself through the ordinary workings of religion, education, politics, law, family, media and so on. This broad definition makes no assumptions regarding truth, illusion, domination, freedom, illumination, science, or class interests. It assumes that all critical perspectives are themselves forms of ideology and, as such, are encumbered by their own pejorative notions and

---

[188] Lee, *Consumer Culture Reborn*, 98.
[189] Lee, *Consumer Culture Reborn*, 106-7.
[190] Lee, *Consumer Culture Reborn*, 99-100.

limiting values.

Consumer Culture and the Ideology of American Individualism

The history of the ideological system that was to provide fertile ground for the germination, growth, and perpetuation of modern consumer culture unfolded in two distinct stages. First, the ideological system that supported the early development of this culture was rooted in Enlightenment notions of an underlying natural order, the perfectibility of the individual, and an inevitable universal human progress based on science and reason. Out of the Enlightenment grew faith in a natural order and emancipating notions of personal liberty and laissez-faire production, commerce, and trade. Here we find the ideological foundations of the Industrial Revolution and of the modern marketplace, which together constitute the intellectual underpinnings of modern capitalism. In a second, quite recent stage of ideological development, the other half of the belief system that today supports today's consumer culture, began to bloom as consumption became more and more relevant and thus has come to stand beside or even replace production in defining Western social relations and personal identity.[191]

The ideology of capitalism began in Europe and quickly established its main thread in America. Grounded in the idea of an intrinsic natural order in all things, America's budding capitalist ideology was rooted in the rational logic of the Enlightenment. By the eighteenth century, the scientific progress that had begun with the Renaissance had firmly impressed on the Western mind the notion that rationally discernible laws governed the natural world. With reason as their Excalibur, the intellectual knights of the Enlightenment set out to slay the dragons of tyranny and superstition and to replace them with natural orders governing the political, social, and economic affairs of men. Inherent in the notion of natural order was the assumption of a clock-like perfection which, when left to its own workings, would beneficially prevail in accordance with the sublime natural clockwork of all things. And inherent in the notion of such intrinsic natural perfection was the notion that the free individual was also perfectible. In America, like nowhere else, enlightened notions of universal human perfection, personal liberty, and the rights of man formed a foundation for the modern concepts of democracy, limited governmental power, social mobility, and laissez-faire economics that were to become the intellectual building blocks of American capitalism.

---

[191] Sassatelli, *Consumer Culture*, 33.

In addition to the lofty ideals of liberty and natural rights, the American mind also embraced more pragmatic visions. With the vast lands of the New World there for the taking, the new national credo of American reason insisted that progress be measured in material terms. Work, thrift, and self-denial became cardinal American virtues and paved the way for capitalism and the industrial revolution, while the accumulation of wealth became the national goal of the rising middle class. All of this was preached under the authority of religion. In America, as in Europe, the Reformation had sounded more than just ecclesiastical chords. Protestantism had voiced a great chorus of earthly material ambition, "condemning leisurely, play-loving activities and substituting the drab ideal of laborious gain." Vernon L. Parrington sums up the American Puritan ethic nicely:

> To labor diligently in the vocation to which one is called of God, it was believed, was to labor under the great Taskmaster's eye, and in the confident hope of eternal reward. No conceivable discipline was better calculated to breed a utilitarian race and create a nation of tradesmen. The immediate result was the emergence of a middleclass... who devoutly believed that the right to rise in the world, to pursue economic well-being in a competitive society, was the most sacred creed of human rights....[192]

And so it was that the lofty ideals of liberty and the utilitarian ethic of hard work blended to create in America a national ideology unlike anything the world had yet beheld. An American inventory of the higher rights of man placed the right to property high on the list, right beside liberty. As Parrington puts it, "The American ideological consensus was bound up in the firm belief that the right of every man to preempt and exploit what he would was synonymous with individual liberty."[193]

This line of thought derived largely from the works of three notable European thinkers of the eighteenth century, James Harrington, John Locke, and Adam Smith, all of whom found a ruling economic mechanism in the natural laws underlying polity and society. In *Oceana*, James Harrington put forward the notion that the true source of political power was economic power, and proposed a government of laws, not men, and a bicameral system of checks and balances to maintain political stability.

John Locke followed Harrington in founding a political theory based on economics, but his approach was more egalitarian. For Locke, although communal property was the natural order of things, nonetheless, following the Puritan tradition, he theorized that men secured the right to private

---

[192] Vernon L. Parrington, *Main Currents in America Thought*, 3 vols. (New York: Harcourt, Brace & World, Inc., 1927) 1:272.

[193] Parrington, *Main Currents In American Thought*, 1:277.

property through work. Locke recognized that securing private property rights separate from the natural commune represented a source of constant friction, and so in his *Second Treatise on Civil Government* he postulated that the preservation and protection of private property was "the great and chief end...of men uniting in commonwealths and putting themselves under the government."

Adam Smith picked up this thread when he published *The Wealth of Nations* in 1776. Smith moved beyond property rights alone, insisting that the great concern of government should be to assist and not to hamper free industry and trade. Like Harrington and Locke before him, Smith teased out notions of a natural economic order underlying government and society. He postulated that free men working unfettered under a government of very limited powers would serve not only their own best interests but also the best interests of society as a whole. In the best Enlightenment tradition, Smith's notion of an "invisible hand of competition" was an extension of the larger notion of the rational benevolence of nature's laws, laws that insisted that, when left alone, nature always worked for the ultimate good.

In all this, James Harrington, John Locke, and Adam Smith had fanned the ideological flames that would fire the future forges of American capitalism, the same forges that would eventually create our modern consumer culture. In the American mind, self-interest and the general welfare were identical owing to a self-regulating mechanism inherent in the natural order of things, and American notions of liberty, laissez-faire trade, free enterprise, and property rights were inexorably entwined. The resulting ideological amalgam contained a revolutionary new element called individualism.

Enlightenment ideologies embracing the automatic, self-directing mechanism of the economic order became the prototype of a free society and formed the jumping off place for the American ideology of individualism. Indeed, like Adam Smith, Americans believed that without a free and natural economy, the state could not function. And following both Locke and Smith, they also insisted that the state's power must be strictly limited because power led to exploitation, destroyed the competitive market economy, severed the bonds between exertion and reward, curtailed justice, and thwarted inventiveness, industry, and progress. Smith believed that a simple system of individual liberties would establish social harmony and foster progress and that the only limiting economic restraint should be what society could achieve for itself through the free actions of its individual members.[194] Embracing this view, America fashioned her unique

---

[194] Yehoshua Arieli, *Individualism and Nationalism in American Ideology* (Cambridge, MA: Harvard University Press, 1964) 118-121.

ideology of individualism using the revolutionary new metals of democracy, popular sovereignty, and the equality of rights among men. Recognizing the distinct essence of the individual man became a distinct ideological end, and the American notion of individualism was fabricated from a devout faith in man's perfectibility, in "his instinctive convictions, his boundless capacity for improvement," and most importantly in his ingrained sense of responsibility for the well-being of society as a whole. Inherent in this faith was the certainty that the desire for justice ruled each individual human will, that each man's self-interest took into account the common good. This is the individualism of "enlightened self-interest," or what Alexis de Tocqueville called "individualism properly understood." Here was a highly idealistic "framework for voluntary social cooperation and for the development of the individual in the utmost freedom."[195]

However, from the very beginning there were those who perceived inherent contradictions in the new American ideology of individualism, contradictions between liberty and equality, between liberty and property, and most notably between self-interest and the public good. While the founding fathers debated checks and balances to guard the new democracy against the threat of a collective "tyranny of the majority," they remained largely unaware of the threat posed by the potential political atomization inherent in American notions of individualism. Tocqueville, however, was quick to grasp the flaw. The ever-insightful French observer clearly saw the potential threat for individual isolation that the American ideology of individualism posed. The self-sufficiency of the individual, his faith in his own reason, and his preoccupation with his own appetites and needs potentially confined each individual to the "solitude of his own heart."[196] In this solitude, Tocqueville knew that each individual reflected on striving to achieve personal independence and that, with the coming of mass society, the isolated individual would become powerless, that personal liberty, which demands personal participation in the affairs of the state, would be destroyed by the individual's myopic, self-serving desire to separately maintain his own independence. The consequence, Tocqueville reasoned, would be "an ever-increasing consolidation of political power and authority and a steady weakening of society. At the end of the process all powers of decision would be transferred to the state."[197]

Such were the perceived dangers of individualism, and yet Tocqueville also saw in the America of the early nineteenth century a path around these

---

[195] Areili, *Individualism and Nationalism*, 191.
[196] Alexis de Tocqueville, *Democracy in America*. (New York: Alfred A. Knopf. 1945), 2:99.
[197] Areili, *Individualism and Nationalism*, 196.

pitfalls. In America, he observed that social and political democracy had evolved to the utmost limit, and in its advanced civil and political liberty America had found the means to successfully combat "the corrosive influences of individualism." Tocqueville theorized that the American success balanced on the existence of institutions so free that they inspired and compelled each individual to take part in public affairs, thus impeding the concentration of political power that individualism might otherwise beget.[198]

What Alexis de Tocqueville failed to understand was the highly idealistic nature of American individualism. In the American mind, self-interest was not the goal of the new national creed of individualism, a free society was the goal; the free pursuit of private interests was simply viewed as a necessary means to that end. Thus, for Americans individualism was a liberating force. In America it was believed that liberty and equality, liberty and property, liberty and self-interest, all went hand-in-hand. True liberty could not exist without equality, without the unfettered right to own and exploit property and to freely pursue one's unique self-interest. Perhaps because of this child-like idealism, the sophisticated European mind of Tocqueville never quite grasp this binding notion so central to the American spirit, and so his insightful evaluations of American individualism went largely ignored in the United States, that is, until 150 years later when consumer culture finally reached maturity and redefined the term "atomization."

Consumer Culture and the Ideology of American Capitalism

With the ideology of individualism first reconciling and then binding together American notions of liberty and property, self-interest and the common good, the young nation set about the job of nation-building confident that the natural workings of a laissez-faire economic system would express both the nation's dedication to personal liberty and uphold the principles of social justice. In fact, in the American mind, one aspect of this ideology justified and supported other. If laissez-faire economics were ever questioned, it was quickly asserted that any meddling with the sanctity and free exchange of private property would constitute a threat to personal liberty. Conversely, any effort to curtail personal liberty was seen as a threat to the continued success of the free economic system. It was this kind of circular logic that allowed American capitalists to disseminate a sweeping political rationale imminently friendly to capitalist growth, to rising

---

[198] Areili, *Individualism and Nationalism*, 197.

corporate America, and to an infantile consumer culture as it took its first wobbly steps in the budding modern American mass society.

More than an idealistic, intellectual ideology rooted in the perfectibility of man and the beneficial workings of natural law, individualism became the living faith of most Americans—both a spiritual faith that proved the harmony of divine natural purposes and a secular, pragmatic faith that envisioned a justly regulated economy, government, and social order. Emerson understood this and spoke of individualism and its dogma not in the language of ideology or philosophy but in terms of a kind of national religion. "Man contains all that is needed to his government within himself," he wrote in 1833,[199] and he clearly believed that man possessed all that was needed for a just society and a robust and egalitarian economy as well. For Emerson, self-government and free trade were voluntary substitutes for force—"natural freedoms" restrained by man's innate sense of "responsibility and morality," the result of the unique "spirit of mankind." According to Emerson, in individualism's bountiful garden, "transport, technology, and science" had "created a new society, based on a community of interests, division of work, and association for common ends."[200] "Property keeps the accounts of the world,"[201] and "Trade goes to make governments insignificant and to bring every kind of faculty of every individual that can in any manner serve any person *on sale*" he wrote, thus converting government into "an Intelligence Office where every man may find what he wishes to buy, and expose what he has to sell."[202] The great Emerson himself was paving the way for the far-reaching commodification that was to sustain the very heartbeat of a blossoming consumer culture.

As the nineteenth century ended, American notions of liberty, individualism, and laissez-faire were becoming deeply engraved on the American soul both as interrelated intellectual and moral constructs and as a unified pragmatic way of life. In this age of rising scientific technology, all that was needed was to clearly identify the scientific mechanism that made the expanding new American ideology so successful and to discover the natural laws at work within the matrix of the so-called "American System." To answer this call came the remarkable theories of Herbert Spencer with their compelling socio-economic spin on the writings of Charles Darwin.

---

[199] Ralph Waldo Emerson, *Journals*, 10 vols. (Boston, Houghton, 1909-14), 3:201.

[200] Areili, *Individualism and Nationalism*, 287.

[201] Ralph Waldo Emerson, quoted in Sacvan Bercovitch, "The Rites of Assent: Rhetoric, Ritual, and the Ideology of American Consensus," in Sam B. Girgus, ed., *The American Self: Myth, Ideology, and Popular Culture* (Albuquerque: University of New Mexico Press, 1981), 33.

[202] Ralph Waldo Emerson, "The Young American," in *The Complete Writings* (New York: William H. Wise & Co., 1929), 1:116.

"Social Darwinism," as Spencer's theories were collectively known, offered a "comprehensive interrogation of economic, political, ethical and philosophical individualism in an all-encompassing and logically consistent scientific theory of irresistible progress."[203] In a codified and orderly reaffirmation of what the country already believed, Spencer repeated, only in different words, the American faith in "a cosmic progress culminating in a perfect adjustment between the individual and society."[204] Here was Emerson's "ideal union in actual individualism," and Jefferson's enlightened notion that individualism went hand in hand with "an elaborate form of mutual dependence."[205] At the core of Spencer's work was "proof" of the natural "compatibility of absolute individual liberty with social cooperation and progress."[206]

Spencer's unflagging popularity in America lasted for three decades, and his theories appealed to every stratum of society. Placing the Darwinian process of natural selection at the center of human experience, Spencer's ideas created social, economic, political, and moral justifications for equal opportunity and social mobility, while explaining the beneficial effects of the private accumulation of wealth and the happy correspondence between success and merit.[207] As a supporter of Charles Darwin's conclusions concerning natural selection, Spencer theorized that the conflicts inherent in the private enterprise system produced higher and higher types of men interacting in more and more advanced and perfected forms of society. Out of this notion grew new and uniquely American ethics and creeds: a widespread belief in the inevitability of Progress, the "Gospel of Wealth," the "Cult of Success," and an unflagging faith in the "American System." These materialist credos helped to identify the ultimate best interests of the masses with competition and with the agendas of industrial and corporate capitalism. Here was an ideology that American capitalists could enthusiastically embrace. Remarking on Spencer's ideas, Andrew Carnegie neatly summed up the view from the high towers of industry: "Not evil, but good, has come to the race from the accumulation of wealth by those who have had the ability and energy to produce it."[208]

By the turn of the twentieth century, the great capitalist American cauldron that contained the ingredients necessary to produce a robust consumer culture had begun to bubble. Patriotic notions of liberty,

---

[203] Areili, *Individualism and Nationalism*, 333.

[204] Areili, *Individualism and Nationalism*, 332.

[205] Herbert Spencer to Horace Seal, quoted in David Duncan, *The Life and Letters of Herbert Spencer* (London: Methuen, 1908), 353.

[206] Areili, *Individualism and Nationalism*, 333.

[207] Areili, *Individualism and Nationalism*, 334.

[208] Andrew Carnegie, quoted in Areili, *Individualism and Nationalism*, 35.

equality, and individualism were beginning to fully meld with notions of opportunity, success, and material wealth. A new and unlovely nationalistic ideal had emerged from the grasping Gilded Age, marrying the concepts of nation, democracy, and industrial enterprise in one compact, unassailable, nationalistic ideology. At the same time, Spencer's Darwinian notions were weaving subtle changes into the American ideology of individualism. Despite Spencer's efforts to prove that, on its course to higher perfection, absolute individual liberty manifested ongoing social cooperation, his theories seemed less than fully convincing when it came to society's duty to see to the well-being of all its members. The ruthless ethic implied in the survival of the fittest, was a long distance from Jefferson's assumption of man's inborn social responsibility and naturally moralistic sense of justice.

The problem was not simply the atomizing nature of American individualism that Tocqueville had feared from the beginning, nor was it the nation's shaky faith in the natural goodness that men possessed even in the pursuit of self-interest. Nor was it simply the onrushing urbanization and alienation of the industrial age. The real problem lay at a much deeper ideological level. According to the sociologist Max Weber, the core logic of modern capitalism was what he called "instrumental reason," an unflaggingly logical, goal-oriented, rational process that was narrowly aimed at the achievement of specific rationally calculated goals. Writing in the first decades of the twentieth century, Weber insisted that modern man had become imprisoned by his own precision and calculability. Indeed, for Weber, the real problem with modern science, technology, industry, and society was the highly focused, standardizing, rational process upon which it had all been built. Individuals in a modern capitalist setting tended to carefully focus the tool of reason, aiming for maximum performance and efficiency in a thought-process that was narrowly fixed on individual problem solving. Such focused rational methods gave no attention to the interests of the wider human whole. Many modern critics have taken up this notion, insisting that "instrumental reason" has accounted for the accumulation of wealth in the West, while at the same time reinforced commodification, dehumanization, and false consciousness, and thereby enslaved workers and consumers alike. Or, put another way, "pursuing problems instrumentally cuts off individuals from everything except their discrete area of self-interest," [209] just as Tocqueville had speculated one hundred years before.

Whether or not the ideal of American individualism was falling victim to the precise logic of "instrumental reason," was a matter for debate. Meanwhile, the nation was being transformed from a wilderness of independent farmers

---

[209] Chris Rojek, *Leisure and Culture* (London: MacMillan Press, Ltd., 2000), 35-6.

into a vast, uniform, urban, middle class nation dedicated to capitalism and to the production of the greatest machine order known to history. In the process, new manners of living emerged, flaunting material conveniences of life, ease of transportation, expanding leisure, and the beginnings of a revolutionary new ethic of consumption. The lofty ideologies of the Enlightenment had melded with the base acquisitive impulses of the Gilded Age to become the handmaidens of American capitalism and nursemaids to the infant consumer culture.[210]

The Ideology of Consumer Culture

By the end of the second decade of the twentieth century, the unique ideology of American capitalism held the entire nation in its grip, and the national dream had shifted its focus to fully embrace the accumulation of wealth. In the American mind, the United States, itself, had come to stand for industrial production, while liberty, that lofty ideal that once stood erect at the pinnacle of American values, had, for many, become little more than a means to a materialistic end. Most Americans agreed with Calvin Coolidge when he declared, "The business of America is business."

As America set about the business of expanding industrial production, the new materialistic ideology of capitalism became a fertile garden for the early growth of American consumerism and consumer culture. In the rich soil of the unprecedented industrial boom of the 1920s, the seeds that would transform the American culture of production into the present American culture of consumption began to take root in the material abundance and widespread personal wealth that flowed from capitalism's apparent triumph. As the 1920s began, per capital income was rising to undreamed of levels, and for the first time consumer credit was being made available to the masses. Having reached the advanced, industrial, so-called "Fordist," corporate stage, American capitalism was filling the marketplace with consumer durables, everything from automobiles to washing machines; and American consumers were buying homes and cars and refrigerators in record numbers, using their new lines of credit. At the same time, the evolving "science" of advertising was perfecting new skills. An advanced new kind marketing was designed not only to stimulate demand and to impregnate products with the ability to convey messages relating to individual identity, but also to modify American culture itself. Advertising contained subtle appeals to a new ideology aimed at helping consumers adapt—that is to say, helping

---

[210] Parrington, *Main Currents In American Thought*, 3:26.

them to culturally and philosophically *become* consumers—and establishing the market as the organizing principle of American life. [211]

A mature consumer culture was beginning to stir, and as it extended its power and its methods, it began to develop its own, distinct, consumption-oriented ideology, which differed from the ideology of capitalist production. Although the culture industry and the well-worn manipulations of production would continue to play a powerful role in creating and sustaining the new ideology of consumer culture, there would come a point at which the fundamental values, mythologies, and iconologies that supported consumer culture's most impressive spectacles and manipulations would come not from these promotional arms of production alone. By the 1960s, a new American ideology was emerging from consumption, itself, and consumerism was cultivating a culture all its own—a culture that was separate from that of production. Nowhere in his vast recorded ponderings had Marx envisioned this kind of bloodless revolution from within. For classical Marxists, the commodity continued to hide the true social relations embodied in production, and most were slow to realize that consumption was creating, and then hiding, social relations of its own making. Marx never dreamed that consumption, and even culture itself, would break free from the all-engrossing grasp of production and that it would wear such spectacular disguises—disguises tailored to deceive and pacify such a sophisticated society. He never imagined that modern consumer culture would require, and in response, independently produce and then perpetuate, its own uniquely blinding ideology.

Up until Marx's time, the development of American capitalism had unfolded in a way that was consistent with the Marxian view of history. To build and sustain the greatest industrial culture in the world, America had carefully constructed a powerful ideology expressly designed to support capitalist production and to validate expanding material progress. To accomplish this end, the national idealistic dedication to liberty and opportunity had been coupled not only to notions of thrift and hard work, but also to a pragmatic faith in material values, worldliness, calculative reason, and entrepreneurial innovation. The resulting ideology of American capitalism produced a society, a government, an economy, and a way of life in which production represented the central organizing principle. To move beyond Marx's ideas and to shift the central focus of American life from production to consumption, the nation had to jettison some of the ideology of capitalism while keeping in place the key cultural pillars that supported production. This would prove dicey. The most fundamental of her cherished

---

[211] Wernick, *Promotional Culture*, 24, 12.

values, norms, personal predilections, and ethics had to be radically altered without disturbing the foundations of the ongoing entrepreneurial order. At the core of these alterations lay the necessity to delicately accomplish a complete reversal of the nation's ideas regarding work and leisure, thrift and spending, luxury and economic value.

At the core of the American work ethic lay individual identity and the national dream of abundance, a vision that dared to assume that, through hard work, frugal accumulation of wealth, and the inevitable progress of modern technology, scarcity might be overcome. By the middle of the twentieth century, it was clear that, for many, this dream of plenty was coming true. However, the resulting economy of abundance presented unforeseen problems. In the American mind, economic value had always been linked to scarcity, which, in turn, had always represented the driving force behind both consumption and production. With the end of scarcity, a new kind of economic motivation was needed to propel the system forward and to ensure continued economic growth. To maintain full production, the nation's concept of economic value had to be completely overhauled, stripped of its intrinsic links to *scarcity* and harnessed to notions of *excess*.[212] The aim of consumption had to be shifted from accumulation to destruction. New needs and new pleasures had to be created, and the new mass media had to be mobilized to "ambush"[213] consumers, stimulating demand for products and services previously thought unnecessary and creating the illusion that completely new products were suddenly indispensable. A new kind of advertising had to be invented to purvey messages, not so much aimed at the marketing of specific products, but at promoting consumption itself as a way of life.[214] As Mike Featherstone puts it, "To control growth effectively and manage the surplus, the only solution was to squander the excess in the form of games, religion, art, wars," gifts, conspicuous consumption, and ubiquitous spectacles of socially symbolic goods.[215] In order to accomplish this, it was necessary for a new culture of the consumer to completely naturalize spending, to convince consumers that shopping, buying, borrowing and spending were an inborn part of our DNA.[216] Such was the mission of the new consumer culture and its media henchmen: to create from the success of the American dream a new ideological economy in which producers manufacture an excess of goods targeted at leisure enjoyments, create new products filled with symbolic meaning and social

[212] Georges Bataille, *The Accursed Share* (New York: Zone Books, 1988).
[213] Cashmore, *Celebrity/Culture*, 68.
[214] Lasch, *Culture of Narcissism*, 72.
[215] Featherstone, *Postmodernism and Consumer Culture*, 22.
[216] Schor, *Born to Buy*, 44.

import, and offer up these products in spectacles of gluttony, overindulgence, and superfluous spending in order to ensure the consumption of capitalism's growing output and propel the entire system forward.

The sweeping cultural upheavals required to create the ideology of American consumer culture would not be accomplished overnight, however the unlovely side effects of industrial production themselves helped to push the process along. Not only had America's industrial success supplied Americans with the abundant means to become a nation of consumers blinded by the consumer-oriented manipulations of the culture industry, but also it had created a disturbing cultural turmoil manifest in urbanization and technological alienation as well as in the growing monotonies in the workplace. Having been snatched from the farm and shut up in the factory, the American worker was suffering a radical identity crisis. The numbing repetitiveness inherent in the division of labor had robbed the work ethic of all inducements save monetary reward and was turning a nation of individuals into a faceless urban mass. On the horns of this dilemma, the American worker had few choices. He or she could withdraw into schizophrenic degeneration, stage the radical revolt that Marx had predicted, or disavow the work ethic altogether and lose himself in a new identity in consumption.

Leisure, Spending, Luxury, and Consumer Culture

At the turn of the twentieth century, most Americans believed that work and thrift were the seminal measures of individual worth, and the nation tenaciously clung to a powerful work ethic and a deeply ingrained asceticism forged in the Puritan mold and annealed on the frontier. However, as the emerging industrial order strode across the continent, American farmers-turned-workers found it increasingly difficult to realize a meaningful sense of moral worth in the dehumanized toil of the factory, where their skills had been seemingly confiscated and subjugated to a numbing kind of mechanical despotism. As a result, the early decades of the new century began to manifest signs of social unrest and class conflict in the form of strikes, employee turnover, and absenteeism.

Henry Ford himself was quick to grasp the problem, and he would offer a uniquely American solution. He would speak to the workers in a language that all Americans understood; he would buy them off. And so began the "Five Dollar Day," a program that raised wages in exchange for submission to the drudgery of mass production. Ford also sought to ensure that his workers used their new-found wealth to build a consumption-oriented lifestyle, and to this end he established a "Sociology Department" within his company and charged it with investigating the home lives and consumption habits of his workers. Other industrialists soon followed suit, thus setting the tone for a gradual shift from a work ethic to a consumption ethic in America. The manipulations of the culture industry followed, and by the 1930s Americans would be on the path to defining themselves not by what they did on the job, but by the lifestyles that they created for themselves with the commodities and activities they consumed in their leisure time.[217] It was the beginning of a national ethical re-orientation that is still ongoing.

Indeed, in America the ethical shift that defines leisure as opposed to work as the primary means of self-identification is far from complete. The ideology of capitalism has always placed leisure second to work in its hierarchy of ideals, and the American work ethic remains deeply entrenched in many areas. For many Americans, notions of leisure and luxury still carry lingering, back-of-the-mind associations with the perceived transgressions and depravities of the idle: bohemianism, hedonism, boundless bodily desires, moral decay, alcoholism, vandalism, crime, and all manner of festering imagined threats to the public good.[218] "Idle hands are the devil's workshop," the saying goes, and this adage still carries weight in heartland America. Today, such a notion is the author of lingering national schizophrenia. As Americans are inexorably drawn to the flame of consumerism and tenderly seduced in consumer culture's spectacular palaces of illusion, there remains a nagging and stubbornly resistant wrinkle in the national psyche. It insists that the overt materialism of unbridled consumption represents a hollow value, that the cycle of work-and-spend is a rat-race powered by a numbing addiction, and that the nation is becoming mesmerized by false values and artificially manufactured needs for vast arrays of luxury goods that have no practical use.

Such prudent values tend to act as moral roadblocks on consumer culture's impulsive highway to unfettered consumption, but by the middle of the twentieth century, many suspected that these barriers would not hold. In his well-known best seller, *The Affluent Society* (1958), John Kenneth Galbraith describes "the process of persuading people to incur debt," as "a part of modern production," and declared that the Puritan ethic was being "overwhelmed by the massive power of modern marketing."[219] Almost twenty years later, in his celebrated book *The Cultural Contradictions of Capitalism* (1976), Daniel Bell described an American culture "no longer concerned with

---

[217] David Gartman, "The Changing American Character: From Work Ethic to Consumption Ethic," http://www.autolife.umd.umich.edu/Design.

[218] Christopher J. Berry, *The Idea of Luxury: A Conceptual and Historical Investigation* (Cambridge: Cambridge University Press, 1994), 232.

[219] Galbraith, *Affluent Society*, cited in Smookler, *Illusion of Choice*, 149-50.

how to work and achieve, but how to spend and enjoy." Although Bell found some signs that many still paid lip service to Protestant ethic, he concluded that the nation had become "primarily hedonistic, and concerned with play, fun, display, and pleasure."[220]

Still, America's long-ingrained Puritanical notions are slow to fade from the national consciousness, even though a clear shift is underway. To counter our stubborn, rigidly moral Puritanical leanings, today's consumer culture supplies compelling justifications. Elaborate rationalizations for hedonistic material excess are wrapped in myths of modern progress that insist "there is nothing wrong with using up resources because we can count of human ingenuity to create new technologies to replace whatever we have destroyed." All the while, such justifications are aimed not at our individual or collective well-being but rather at the infinite expansion of the economic system.

From the beginning, it was clear that capitalism was premised upon the primacy of desire, and in a cultural logic so frankly constructed, luxury, as a creature of desire, no longer appears to represent a corruption.[221] Meanwhile, as work becomes more automated, drearier, and less satisfying, its value as a source of individual dignity, social status, and self-worth is diminished. As a result, work surrenders some of its ability to signify meaning to the self and to others. This allows consumer culture and its media-henchmen to persistently challenge the dominant assumption that social status, self-worth, self-discovery, and self-transformation are accomplished through work, and to flaunt the rich array of exotic individual identity choices that are for sale in the marketplace. The consumption ethic first appears at the point where commodities are mediated to the public, where future markets are invited to meet existing products, where buyers and sellers converge in the dreamscapes of glossy magazines, commercials, and mail-order catalogues.[222]

Today, most Americans tend to judge a person's vocation by the amount of money it generates rather than by the associated status, achievements, productiveness, or any other intrinsic value that work might manifest. Modern consumer culture continually seeks to naturalize and reinforce the notion that leisure is no longer an activity pursued for its own sake. Rather, this culture insists that, when ideologically is linked to consumption, one's leisure activities and purchases supply the building blocks for new, modern,

[220] Daniel Bell, *The Cultural Contradictions of Capitalism* (New York: Basic Books, 1976), cited in Schmookler, *Illusion of Choice*, 149.

[221] Berry, *Idea of Luxury*, 233.

[222] Dick Hebdige, "A Report on the Western Front: Postmodernism and the Politics of Style," in Chris Jenks, ed. *Cultural Reproduction* (London and New York: Routledge, 1993), 69-103.

personal identities. In short, the transition from a work ethic to a leisure ethic in America is being accomplished by discrediting work as a purveyor of intrinsic reward, and by presenting it only as means to achieve leisure, which in turn gains status when viewed as a reward for work. So, the cycle begins: first, work and save; then, work and spend; and finally, work *in order* to spend, and through consumption, to be.

To fully achieve the kind of fundamental shift in the national ethic required for the total triumph of consumer culture, Americans must first be convinced that the goodness they once found in work can now be found in leisure and consumption. Inherent in such a shift is the creation of a new value system in which leisure, spending, and debt are completely de-vilified and the notion that luxury is now cleansed of any previous decadent associations. However, more is needed than the complete "demoralization" of leisure and luxury. In order flourish, the new culture of the commodity must entrench consumption as a new American "sphere of action" universally valorized by a new national "order of justification."[223] Just as the new nation created the ideology of American capitalism by fusing the ideals of liberty and property with notions of laissez-faire economics and industrial progress, so she is now employing the same ideals to create, and at the same time to valorize, a national ideology of leisure and consumption. Marrying the same cherished ideals of American liberty and property, this time with notions of personal economic freedom, liberal borrowing, uninhibited consumption, and unfettered spending, America is dusting off the ideology of individualism and the national faith in the self-correcting nature of the pursuit of self-interest and giving it a new twist. The focus now shifts from the freedom to exploit and to accumulate and concentrates squarely upon the freedom to recreate and to consume. In the process, the work ethic is not so much destroyed as it is demoted to a mere means to the fulfillment of the new ethic of consumption. It is an ingenious solution to a knotty problem. In the contemporary American mind, recreation and consumption, like work and production before them, are being deftly and inseparably linked to notions of patriotism, democracy, and liberty, until abundant leisure, unfettered borrowing, and the free consumption of even the most frivolous of luxuries are fashioned to represent basic rights and the very cornerstones of individual freedom itself.

Thus, modern American consumer culture first assails us with the notion that liberty, personal freedom, and self determination are now articulated by choices in the marketplace and by the unfettered option to buy anything we

---

[223] Luc Boltanski and Laurent Thévenot, *De la Justification: Les Économies de la Grandeur* (Paris: Gallimard, 1991), quoted in Sassatelli, *Consumer Culture*, 41.

want. It then seduces us with the perception of yet another kind of freedom: the freedom to re-create ourselves by fashioning unique new individual lifestyles from the vast assortment of products and leisure activities that are paraded before us in compelling spectacles of illusion. Once it gains a foothold, the ideology of consumer culture is self-perpetuating. There are those who liken it to "a black hole in our social universe, a force warping the course of our society's development" by bending our values toward materialism. Such a view insists that over time the movement of American ideological values from spiritual or idealistic to material constitutes evidence of the power of the commodity "to shape society according to its own logic."[224] Along the way, a culture of consumption is being created in America, a culture so powerful, so flexible, that it appears to assimilate and then absorb all resistance—a culture that first invisibly and irresistibly replaces *being* with *having*, then invisibly seeks to reduce *having* to *appearing*.[225]

---

[224] Schmookler, *Illusion of Choice*, 128.
[225] DeBord, *The Society of the Spectacle*, Thesis Number 17.

CHAPTER NINE: AMERICAN INDIVIDUALISM AND THE PARADOX OF
CONSUMER CULTURE

A Chronicle of American Individualism

Despite the irresistible allure of the new materialism, the old individualism still lingers—hangs on, refuses to give in. For two centuries, the free individual has stood at the ideological center of American capitalist culture. From the beginning, the complex national ideology of individualism gathered unto itself all those ideals that we have come to call American: liberty, democracy, equality, property, laissez-affaire economics, the rule of law, and the American way of life. It has unswervingly rejected all frameworks of collective identification and warily mistrusted the power of the state. Contained within the American concept of individualism is the surety that the free democratic society from which it arose has universal significance. Unlike Old-World connotations of the term, which suggested selfishness, anarchy, apathy toward the common good, and reflexive self-gratification, in the idealistic, young, American mind, individualism pointed to self-realization, moral freedom, pure liberty, and the perfectibility and dignity of man.[226] Seen to be the revolutionary amalgam of the isolation of the New World experience, the hardships of the frontier, and a steadfast national faith in self-reliance, throughout the nineteenth century, American individualism expressed itself in "abundant energy of action, ideals of unrestrained individual freedom, the capacity for organization and daring enterprise, and the belief in a free competitive economy."[227]

---

[226] Arieli, *Individualism and Nationalism*, 186-89.
[227] Edwin Lawrence Godkin, "Aristocratic Options of Democracy, in *Problems of Modern Democracy: Political and Economic Essays* (New York: Charles Scribner's Sons, 1896), cited in

As the twentieth century began, serious threats to American individualism began to materialize. The frontier was at an end, great cities had begun to sprawl, and a nation of independent farmers was being transformed into a nation of faceless factory workers and clerks. Armed with the dual swords of conformity and alienation, the armies of the Modern Age appeared to be plowing under the old individualism. The socializing trends of the Progressive Era and later of the New Deal were logical expressions of a new American temperament, reflecting "the decline of individualism and the growth of social responsibility that could be noted in law, education, business...legislation," and philosophy.[228] Indeed, a philosophical shift appeared to be underway, an ideological attempt to replace the salvation of the individual as the central focus of American thought and put in its place the reconstruction of society.[229]

At the same time, the armies of the commodity were massing for battle. By mid-century, the vast, subversive, materialist juggernaut of mounting American consumer culture appeared poised for an assault on the beleaguered forces of individualism. Here was an insurgent army that attacked from within. Its weapons were unconventional—fantasy, simulation, media, spectacle, and illusion—and its aim was not to destroy American individualism, but to corrupt it, to rob it of its ability of coalesce, to strip it of its sense of the common good and its remarkable capability to resist its own inherent atomizing tendencies. By the early 1960s, the forces of consumption were sweeping away everything in their path, commodifying, seducing, and atomizing all who stood before their relentless advance. The real battle had at last begun, and it continues today, pitting the waning forces of the old idealistic American individualism against the boundless advancing commodity armies of modern consumer culture. This book has been an attempt to chronicle that battle.

Individualism and Ambiguity in Consumer Culture

Just as the individual once stood as the center of young idealistic American mind, the individual now stands at the center of American consumer culture. At first, it was thought that this commodity culture dominated and debased the individual, closing off all avenues of resistance in its blinding, self-perpetuating control of all who entered its glittering web of illusions. However, today there are those who question the pervasiveness

Arieli, *Individualism and Nationalism*, 196-7.

[228] Henry Steele Commager, *The American Mind: An Interpretation of American Thought and Character Since the 1880s* (New Haven: Yale University Press, 1950), 176-7.

[229] Commager, *American Mind*, 100.

of this domination. Some observers go so far as to suggest that the choices available to us represent a growing diversity of *expanding* freedoms in an "acknowledgement of the right of individuals to enjoy whatever pleasures they desire without encountering prudery or moral censure."[230] Nonetheless, the question remains. Does our consumer culture free us or enslave us? Do the new lifestyles we create by rummaging in the marketplace replenish our lost individualism and create a new world of tolerance; or does the market culture atomize us and rob us of our ability to coalesce and our sense of duty to the common good? Can we really reinvent ourselves and our individualism in the commodity, or is it just a hollow illusion created by a depthless culture in which "all values have been trans-valued" and a thoroughly commercialized "art has triumphed over reality?"[231] Or could the answer be both?

As we have seen, modern consumer culture is always busy blurring boundaries, creating ambiguities, and destroying the sturdy and well-defined partitions that separated the distinct compartments of a once-orderly reality. For example, we have seen that it fuses high art with popular culture, obscures social relations in the spectacle the commodity, confuses copies with originals, mistakes images for the actual, and renders fantasy indistinguishable from reality. When we structure our identities using the products and experiences we find in the marketplace, the dual nature of American individualism becomes blurred. While we may indeed revitalize our individualism in consumption, the individualism we create is often of the wrong kind: that is, the selfish, hollow, hedonistic individualism that is heedless of its obligation to see to the good of the whole. And yet, amid the glitter and glitz there remain pockets of resistance, "temporary communities,"[232] "liberating spaces of self-expression."[233] While it is clear that consumer culture seeks to reproduce the selfish kind of individualism that defines liberty as simply the freedom to buy whatever one wants, at the same time, it is equally clear that the attending popular culture still contains myriad sources of resistance and thousands of paths to individual rebellion. Many of these roads still lead to individually perceived notions of the "common good," each centering on its own narrow agenda: the environment, gay rights, civil liberties, smoker's rights, whatever. In truth, American consumer culture does not destroy either kind of individualism. While it universally attempts to perpetuate the grasping, selfish kind, it also allows the idealistic strain to exist. In so doing, it blurs the distinction between the

---

[230] Featherstone, *Consumer Culture and Postmodernism*, 84.

[231] Featherstone, *Consumer Culture and Postmodernism*, 85.

[232] Michel Maffesoli, "Jeux de Masques: Postmodernism and the Megapolis," *Threshold IV*, 1, cited in Featherstone, *Consumer Culture and Postmodernism*, 101.

[233] Lee, *Consumer Culture Reborn*, 50.

two. It allows protest, but carefully keeps individual movements separate while it commodifies them, assimilating the style and the substance of revolt into the vast marketplace of commodities. For example, before the 1960s ended, *Hair* became a musical peace symbol and it adorned everything from automobile bumpers to children's lunchboxes. Later, the outrage of "punk" *became* the rage. And so it went. And so it still goes. Consumer culture is willing to give us anything we desire—save the real power to meaningfully unite and significantly amend the status quo or to stand in the way of its own reproduction and self-perpetuation.

The blurring of the two faces of American individualism reveals the true nature of American consumer culture. No matter how we choose to examine it, in all its various fields of operation—cultural, social, economic, moral, ideological, or political—it manifests a contradiction. Once opposing evaluations are sucked in, commodified, and re-broadcast for widespread consumption, the inevitable effect is a blurring of all arguments, facts, realities, ideals, and hopes until the entrenched positions at either end of any debate disappear into a dynamic swirl of hype, hyperbole, and spectacle. Consumer culture does not polarize our debates regarding its true nature into stark blacks and whites. In fact, in its illusory fantasy-worlds, the combination of black and white does not even produce grey, but rather blinding, Day-Glo flashes of color and light. For all its blending, our examinations of American consumer culture supply neither answers nor solutions, they create only ambiguities, which give rise to the endless ironies that characterize our world.

For example, we began by saying that, when it comes to examining consumption, most scholars use the Marxian view as a jumping off point. In Marx's fertile mind, consumption, and even culture itself, were artifacts of production. Latter day Marxists have pointed to the culture industry as a living example of the power of the persuasive manipulations achieved by the forces of production. In the so-called culture industry, advertising, film, and television have perpetuated a myth of success so compelling that it induces us to passionately embrace the very ideology that enslaves us. Although today's consumer culture clearly embraces and exploits these powerful manipulations of production, it is not so one-dimensional as to rely solely on a single source of power. It also finds autonomous power in consumption, power that creates and then masks its own unique social relations—relations that are different from those created and masked by production. In revealing the autonomous powers of culture and consumption, consumer culture stands Marxism on its head. While it embraces of the powers of production simultaneously with the powers of consumption, in no way does it ever consider these powers distinct. American consumer culture exercises only blended strength and renders only blended results. It is neither the exclusive territory of production nor of consumption, neither a realm of absolute domination nor of universal emancipation, neither totally rational nor totally irrational. Modern consumer culture abhors dichotomy and thrives on blended patterns and relations that are infinitely more "complex, nuanced, and opaque."[234]

The Paradox of Consumer Culture

Nowhere is this ambiguity and complexity clearer than in our examinations of the diverse lifestyles and personal identities that we create for ourselves in the consumer culture. Here the central question revolves around the quality and the long-term stability of these identities. In the broadest terms, studies point to two scenarios. On one hand, it appears that personal identities constructed solely from the flimsy lumber of a hollow materialism will, themselves, ultimately prove hollow and fragile. More specifically, this school of thought holds that identities we create using the signs and symbols produced by advertising and by the culture industry are as fickle and as unstable as the accelerating pace of fashion itself. We embrace "cutting edge" fashions to differentiate ourselves from the group only to cast them off when they become so popular that they lose their distinguishing qualities. American consumer culture warmly embraces all who attempt self-realization using such transient symbols as "ideal consumers," for they propel this culture toward its only real goal, the growth and perpetuation of the system. Clearly, this is a form of domination, and any identities built on this kind of constantly shifting materialism are likely to prove unstable and ultimately unworkable.

On the other hand, there are those who suggest that some of the symbols we garner from the commodities we purchase can be emancipating. However, consumer culture closely controls such emancipation by commodifying, watering down, and finally assimilating countercultures and revolts of all sorts. Nonetheless, a few subversive and emancipating spaces remain, but in most cases these do not originate in the marketplace. They are our own creations. Once we purchase a commodity and it leaves the marketplace, we can shape it into something very personal, something unique, even into something subversive—something that resists consumer culture's endless spectacles of fashion and tend, something that sparks dreams of an alternative future. Clearly there is an element of freedom here, however, this

---

[234] Sassatelli, *Consumer Culture*, 195.

kind of freedom derives from meanings transferred to commodities after they are purchased, that is, it originates outside of the marketplace. It seems likely that the motivation to attach this kind of highly personal, and often subversive symbolism to purchased goods and services comes from vestiges of older identities that have not yet been destroyed by the onslaught of the forces of an older, regimenting Modernity or by our consumer culture itself. Most often, such creations flow from vestigial remains of the old individualism, from stubborn remnants of the work ethic, or from the lingering relics of our past spirituality.

In another example, some scholars have opined that the expanding landscape of choice within the marketplace represents a movement toward diversity and perhaps even toward increased tolerance. It is certainly true that consumer culture does embrace diversity and tolerance, at least to the extent that they broaden consumption and expand the system. However, it offers only choices that further such expansion. In this regard, it offers no real freedom of choice, only illusions of choice.

Amid all the blending and blurring, all the contradictions and ambiguities, the question remains: are we really free to choose? Does consumer culture ultimately free us or enslave us? As the custodian of the modern marketplace, it offers us spectacular mechanisms for channeling individual human choices. As individuals, we enjoy a breathtaking rage of immediate choices, and in turn, the market is quickly shaped by the choices we make. Thus, in one way, the culture of consumption seems uniquely sensitive to our immediate needs. And yet, at the same time, the entire system appears blind to our most pressing long-term requirements. Ignoring vital societal and ecological issues, today's American consumer culture focuses on its own growth and reproduction. In so doing, it channels our choices. Thus, ironically, amid the bounty of so many choices, it creates "a world in which no one can choose," and we find our real destinies controlled by an automatic system that only moves society and the physical world in directions that are compatible with its own narrow goals."[235] Our actions, even un-coerced, are not necessarily free. Invisibly, modern American consumer culture imposes taxing burdens on our inter-connectedness, our ability to politically and socially coalesce and to join together for the long term common good. Its hedonistic fascinations, atomize us, dismantle all collectives, and channel our individual energies into materialist fascinations of its own choosing.[236] Our consumer culture may allow us to choose our lifestyles and even our identities, but it stands in the way when it comes to choosing our destiny.

---

[235] Schmookler, *Illusion of Choice*, 11, 76.
[236] Schmookler, *Illusion of Choice*, 76.

Perhaps the most compelling example of American consumer culture's myopic manipulations is its total disregard for environmental concerns. Today, all of us are quickly coming to realize that enormous sacrifices are going to be necessary to check the advance of pollution, global warming, and environmental corruptions of all sorts. However, our consumer culture is blind to such concerns. Clean air, clean water, urban planning, and global cooperation are not consistent with uninterrupted economic expansion, and so consumer culture perpetuates a myth of technological progress that insists that there is nothing wrong with fouling the environment and using up resources because technology will devise systems to replace whatever we destroy.[237] Such reckless, environmental insensitivity typifies consumer culture's disregard for the public realm. The logic of consumerism insists that human welfare is synonymous only with economic expansion, and thus it turns a blind eye to anything that might stand in the path of its own prosperity and growth and fails to take into account the long-term consequences of its shortsighted strategies. Atomizing individuals in spectacular rituals of consumption, it creates superfluous private abundance while at the same time it obstructs communal organization and impoverishes the public realm. In short, modern consumer culture fails to recognize the vital web of our interdependency. It alienates us "from any sense of the Whole of which we are apart."[238] The single focus of today's consumer culture is not the welfare of the individuals within the system but the welfare of the system itself.

There are those who argue that all the institutions that make up the culture of the consumer—corporations, businesses, governments, media concerns, and so on—are controlled by free individuals. However, such an argument fails to grasp this culture's power. The powerful individuals, who function as the cultural custodians, are created, trained, and then hand-picked by the system. To be selected by the system, these leaders must embrace only the ideology of the system. An ideology created by the culture that they maintain. They thus exercise no real autonomous power. The CEO of an international corporation may appear to have made his or her way to the top through creative individual initiative, but only those who meet every one of our consumer culture's strict qualifications are ever put in a position to vie for such a post. Likewise, all the candidates whose names appear on ballots are handpicked by the culture. The unshakable logic of the system is such that only candidates dedicated to the culture of consumption's unswerving agenda of consumption and growth can entertain any chance of political success. These are the politics of modern consumer culture—polemics in

---

[237] Schmookler, *Illusion of Choice*, 105.
[238] Schmookler, *Illusion of Choice*, 301.

which real power lies not with the people within the system, but with the system itself.[239] Again, the choices offered to us represent no real choice at all, only the illusion of choice.

The American republic was designed to resist tyranny, to walk the narrow path between the will of the majority and the rights of the individual, to balance on the razor-edged boundaries that divide individual liberty and community, equality and property. However, for all the checks and balances the founding fathers built into our system, none was designed to guard against the insidious and unforeseen tyranny of our own material success. No one imagined that we would all become willing conspirators in a plot to undermine our own freedom, a paradoxical plot that would employ our own cherished ideals to covertly destroy our cherished liberty. Who among us would have suspected that in achieving the American Dream, we would create a pervasive national consciousness that defined life solely in the material aspirations of that dream? Under the banners of liberty, democracy, equality, diversity, tolerance, and individualism, American consumer culture threatens our collective social imagination, separates us from any sense of a common destiny, robs us of our power to coalesce, and blinds us to human possibilities that extend beyond the current concept of the good life.

Here is the heart-wrenching American irony: lost in a hyper-real spectacle of commodification and aesthetic illusion and oblivious to our own servitude, we tenaciously embrace the ideology of the tyrannical system that enslaves us.

---

[239] Schmookler, *Illusion of Choice*, 228.

BIBLIOGRAPHY

Adorno, Theodor W. and Max Horkheimer. "The Culture Industry: Enlightenment as Mass Deception." In Schor and Holt, ed. *The Consumer Society Reader*, 2000, 4-19.

Althusser, Louis. "Ideology and the State." In *Lenin and Philosophy and Other Essays*. London: Verso, 1971.

Arieli, Yehoshua. *Individualism and Nationalism in American Ideology*. Cambridge, MA: Harvard University Press, 1964.

Bataille, Georges. *The Accursed Share*. New York: Zone Books, 1988.

Baudelaire, Charles. *Les Fleurs du Mal*. Translated by Richard Howard. Boston: David R. Godine, 1982.

_____ "The Painter of Modern Life," in *The Painter of Modern Life and Other Essays*. Oxford: Phaidon Press, 1964.

Baudrillard, Jean. *The Intelligence of Evil or the Lucidity Pact*. Oxford: Berg, 2005.

_____ *Passwords*. London and New York: Verso, 2003.

_____ *The Perfect Crime*. London and New York: Verso, 1996.

_____ "Simulacra and Simulations." In *Selected Writings*. Edited by Mark Poster. Stanford: Stanford University Press, 1988, 166-84.

_____ *Simulations*, New York: Semiotext, 1983.

Bakhtin, Mikhail. *Rabelais and his World*. Cambridge, MA: MIT Press, 1968.

Bell, Daniel. "Forward, 1976." In *The Coming of Post-Industrial Society*. New York: Basic Books, 1976.

Belsey, Catherine. *Critical Practice*. London: Methuen, 1980.

Benjamin, Walter. *Gesammelte Schriften*. Edited by Rolf Tiedemann and Herman Schweppenäuser. Frankfurt: Suhrkamp Verlag, 1972.

_____*Charles Baudelaire: A Lyric Poet in the Era of High Capitalism*. Translated by Harry Zohn. London: Verso, 1983.

_____*Illuminations*. Edited by Hannah Arendt. New York: Harcourt, Brace and World, 1968.

_____"Literary History and the Study of Literature." In *Selected Writings*, 1999.

_____"Paris, Capital of the Nineteenth Century." Translated by Howard Eiland. In *The Writer of Modern Life*, 2006.

_____"Paris of the Second Empire in Baudelaire." Translated by Harry Zohn. In *The Writer of Modern Life*, 2006.

_____*Selected Writings*. Edited by Marcus Bullock and Michael W. Jennings. Translated by Harry Zohn. Cambridge MA: Harvard University Press, 1999.

_____*The Writer of Modern Life: Essays on Charles Baudelaire*. Edited by Michael W. Jennings. Translated by Howard Eiland, Edmund Jephcott, Rodney Livingstone, and Harry Zohn. Cambridge, MA: The Belknap Press of Harvard University, 2006.

_____ "The Work of Art in the Age of Mechanical Reproduction." In *Illuminations*, 1968, 219-253.

Bercovitch, Dacvan. "The Rites of Assent: Rhetoric, Ritual, and the Ideology of American Consensus." In *The American Self: Myth, Ideology, and Popular Culture*. Edited by Sam B. Girgus. Albequerque: University of New Mexico Press, 1981.

Berger, John. *Ways of Seeing*. London: BBC/Penguin, 1972.

Berry, Christopher J. *The Idea of Luxury: A Conceptual and Historical Investigation*. Cambridge: Cambridge University Press, 1994.

Best, Steven and Douglas Kellner. *Postmodern Theory: Critical Interrogations*. New York: The Guilford Press, 1991.

Boltanski, Luc and Laurent Thévenot. *De La Justification: Les Économies del la Granduer*. Paris: Gallimard, 1991.

Bourdieu, Pierre. *Distinction: A Social Critique of the Judgment of Taste*. London: Routledge, 1984.

Bronfen, Elizabeth. "Celebrating Catastrophe." In *Angelaki: Journal of Theoretical Humanities*, Vol. 7, No. 2, 2002, 175-86.

Brooker, Peter and Will Brooker, ed. *Postmodern Afterimages: A Reader in Film, Television, and Video*. London: Arnold, 1997.

Bukatman, Scott. "Who Programs You? The Science Fiction of the Spectacle." In Brooker and Brooker, ed., *Postmodern Afterimages*, 1997.

Buck-Moss, Susan. "Benjamin's *Passagen-Werk*." New German Critique, No. 29, 1983.

Cahoone, Lawrence, ed., *From Modernism to Postmodernism: An Anthology*. Second Edition. Malden, MA: Blackwell Publishing, 2003.

_____"Max Weber," in Cahoone, *From Modernism to Postmodernism*, 2003.

Caldwell, John. *Televisuality: Style, Crisis, and Authority in American Television*. New Brunswick, NJ: Rutgers University Press, 1995.

Cashmore, Ellis. *Celebrity/Culture*. New York: Routledge, 2006.

Commager, Henry Steele. *The American Mind: An Interpretation of American Thought and Character Since the 1880s*. New Haven: Yale University Press, 1950.

Cook, Deborah. *The Culture Industry Revisited: Theodor W. Adorno on Mass Culture*. Landham MD: Rowand and Littlefield, 1996.

Creeber, Glen "Decoding Television: Issues of Ideology and Discourse." In *Televisions: An Introduction to Studying Television*. Edited by Glen Creeber. BFI: London, 2006.

DeBord, Guy. *The Society of the Spectacle*. Detroit: Black and Red, 1967.

Downing David B. and Susan Bazargan. "Image and Ideology: Some Preliminary Histories and Problems." In *Image and Ideology in Modern/Postmodern Discourse*. Edited by David B. Browning and Susan Bazargan. Albany, NY: State University Press of New York, 1991.

Duncan, David. *The Life and Letters of Herbert Spencer*. London: Methuen, 1908.

Emerson, Ralph Waldo. *Journals*. 10 vols. Edited by Edward Waldo Emerson and Waldo Emerson Forbes. Boston: Houghton, 1909-1914.

_____ "The Young American," in *The Complete Writings*. 8 vols. New York: William H. Wise & Co., 1929.

Ewen, Stuart and Elizabeth Ewen. *Channels of Desire*. New York: McGraw Hill, 1982.

Featherstone, Mike. *Consumer Culture and Postmodernism*. London and Thousand Oaks, CA: SAGE Publications, 1991.

Foucault, Michel. "What is Enlightenment?" In *The Foucault Reader*. Edited by Paul Rabinow. Harmondsworth, Penguin, 1986.

Fisk, John. *Understanding Popular Culture*. London: Unwin Hyman, 1989.

Gabler, Neal. *Life, the Movie: How Entertainment Conquered Reality*. New York, Knopf, 1998.

Galbraith, John Kenneth. *The Affluent Society*. London: Andre Deutsch, 1958.

Godkin, Edwin Lawrence. "Aristocratic Options of Democracy." In *Problems of Modern Democracy: Political and Economic Essays*. New York: Charles Scribner's Sons, 1896.

Haug, Wolfgang F. *Critique of Commodity Aesthetics*. Oxford: Polity Press, 1986.

Hebdige, Dick "A Report on the Western Front: Postmodernism and the Politics of Style." In Jenks, *Cultural Reproduction*, 1993, 69-103.

Jameson, Fredric. *Postmodernism: The Cultural Logic of Late Capitalism*. Durham: Duke University Press, 1991.

_____ "Postmodernism and Consumer Society." In *Postmodern Culture*. Edited by Hal Foster. London: Pluto Press, 1985.

Jenks, Chris. "Introduction: The Analytical Bases of Cultural Reproduction." In Jenks, *Cultural Reproduction*, 1993.

_____ ed., *Cultural Reproduction*. London and New York: Routledge, 1993.

Jennings, Michael W. "Introduction." In Walter Benjamin, *The Writer of Modern Life*, 2006.

Kellner, Douglas. "Media Culture and the Triumph of the Spectacle." In King, *The Spectacle of the Real*, 2005.

_____"Theorizing/Resisting McDonaldization: A Multiperspective Approach," at "Illuminations: The Critical Theory Website," http://www.uta.edu/illuminations/Kell30.htm.

King, Geoff ed. *The Spectacle of the Real: From Hollywood to Reality TV and Beyond*. Bristol, UK: Intellect, 2005.

Klein, Naomi. *No Logo*. London: Flamingo, 2002.

Kooistra, Paul. "Criminals As Heroes: Linking Symbol to Structure." In *Caliber: Journals of the University of California Press*, 1990, Vol. 13, No. 2, 217–239.

Lanham, Richard A. *The Economics of Attention: Style and Substance in the Age of Information*. Chicago and London: The University of Chicago Press, 2006.

Lasch, Christopher. *The Culture of Narcissism: American Life in an Age of Diminishing Expectations*. London: Abacus, 1980.

_____*The True and Only Heaven: Progress and Its Critics*. New York: W. W. Norton, 1991.

Lee, Martyn J. *Consumer Culture Reborn: The Cultural Politics of Consumption*. Routledge: London and New York, 1993.

Lévy, Pierre. *Cyberculture*. Translated by Robert Bononno. Minneapolis and London, University of Minnesota Press, 2001.

Lowenthal, Leo. "The Triumph of Mass Idols," (1944). In *Literature, Popular Culture and Society*. Palo Alto, Ca: Pacific, 1961, 109-40.

Lukács, Georg. *History and Class Consciousness: Studies in Marxist Dialectics*. 1923. Translated by Rodney Livingstone. Cambridge, MA: MIT Press, 1971.

Lyotard, Jean-François. *The Postmodern Condition*. Minneapolis: University of Minnesota Press, 1984.

_____*The Postmodern Condition*. Manchester: Manchester University Press, 1984.

Marshall, P. David. *Celebrity and Power: Fame in Contemporary Culture*. Minneapolis: University of Minnesota Press, 1997.

Marx, Karl and Friedrich Engels. *Manifesto of the Communist Party*. Translated by Samuel Moore. In Tucker, *The Marx-Engles Reader*, 473-83.

_____*Capital: A Critique of the Political Economy*, 3 vols. Moscow: Progress Publishers, 1977.

_____*Capital, The Communist Manifesto and Other Writings*, Abridged Edition. Edited by Julian Borchardt. New York: The Modern Library, 1932

_____ *The Marx-Engels Reader*, Second Edition. Edited by Robert C. Tucker. New York: Norton, 1978.

_____*The German Ideology*, Progress Publishers, Moscow, 1964.

McCracken, Grant. *Culture and Consumption II: Markets, Meaning and Brand Management*. Bloomington: Indiana University Press, 2005.

McKendrick, Neil. "Commercialization and the Economy." In Niel McKendrick, John Brewer, and J.H. Plumb, ed. *The Birth of Consumer Society: The Commercialization of Eighteenth-Century England*. Bloomington: Indianan University Press, 1982.

Neimark, Jill. "The Culture of Celebrity." In *Psychology Today*, May/June, 1995, 54-7, 87-90.

Parrington, Vernon L. *Main Currents in America Thought*, 3 vols. New York: Harcourt, Brace & World, Inc., 1927.

Patton, Phil. "Sell the Cookstove if Necessary, but Come to the Fair." In *Smithsonian*, June, 1993, 24:38-50.

Rojek, Chris. *Leisure and Culture*. London: MacMillan Press, Ltd., 2000.

Ritzer, George. *The McDonaldization of Society*, 2nd Edition. Thousand Oaks, CA: Pine Forge Press, 1996.

_____*Enchanting a Disenchanted World: Revolutionizing the Means of Consumption*. London: Pine Forge Press, 1999, 84-85.

Sassatelli, Roberta. *Consumer Culture: History, Theory, and Politics*. Los Angeles: SAGE Publications, 2007.

Schickel, Richard. *Intimate Strangers: The Culture of Celebrity*. Garden City, NJ: Doubleday and Company, Inc., 1985.

Schmookler, Andrew Bard. *The Illusion of Choice*. Albany: The State University of New York, 1993.

Schor, Juliet B. *Born to Buy: The Commercialized Child and the New Consumer Culture*. New York: Scribner, 2004.

_____and Douglas B. Holt, ed. *The Consumer Society Reader*. New York: The New Press, 2000.

Shusterman, Richard. "Postmodern Aestheticism: A New Moral Philosophy?" In *Theory, Culture, Society*, Vol. 5, No. 2, 1988, 337-55.

Simmel, Georg. "Fashion." In *International Quarterly*, vol. 10, No. 1, October 1904, 130-155. Reprinted in *American Journal of Sociology*, vol. 62, No. 6, May 1957, 541-558.

Slater, Don. "Going Shopping: Markets, Crowds, and Consumption." In Jenks, *Cultural Reproduction*, 1993.

Sontag, Susan. "Notes on Camp." In *Against Interpretation*. New York : Farrar, Straus & Giroux, 1966.

Stearns, Peter N. *Consumerism in World History: The Global Transformation of Desire*. New York And London; Routledge, 2006.

Street, John. "Celebrity Politicians: Popular Culture and Political Representation." In *The British Journal of Politics and International Relations*, 2004 Vol. 6, 435-452.

Thompson, John. *The Media and Modernity: A Social Theory of the Media*. Cambridge: Polity, 1995.

Tocqueville, Alexis de. *Democracy in America*. 2 vols. Edited by Phillips Bradley. New York: Alfred A. Knopf. 1945.

Twitchell, James. "Two Cheers for Materialism," 1999. In Schor and Holt, ed. *The Consumer Society Reader*, 2000.

Umphlett, Wiley Lee. *From Television to the Internet: Postmodern Visions of American Media Culture in the Twentieth Century*. Madison, WI: Fairleigh Dickinson University Press, 2006.

Veblen, Thorstein. *The Theory of the Leisure Class*, 1899. London: MacMillan, 1994.

Weber, Max. *The Protestant Ethic and the Spirit of Capitalism*, 1904. London: Allen and Unwin, 1930.

Wernick, Andrew. *Promotional Culture: Advertising, Ideology, and Symbolic Expression*. London: SAGE Publications, 1991.

Williams, Rosalind H. *Dream Worlds: Mass Consumption in Late Nineteenth Century France*. Berkley: California University Press, 1982.

Index

A

Adorno, Theodor, 38-40, 67, 70
Aestheticization, 64, 96, 99, 103
American Dream, 16, 54, 120, 134
Americanization, 18
Arcades Project, The, 37, 38

B

Bakhtin, Mikhail, 26
Baudelaire, Charles, 25, 33-38, 102
Baudrillard, Jean, 44-46, 64, 65, 68, 77, 96, 97, 99, 106
Bell, Daniel, 41, 42, 44, 45, 122, 123
Benjamin, Walter, 25, 31, 33-38, 42, 70, 100, 102
Brands, 10, 14, 16, 18-21, 32, 53, 66, 74, 85-87, 108
Brand Identity, 53
BrandsMart, 10, 18-20

C

Camp, 12, 17, 90, 97
Carnegie, Andrew, 116
Celebrities, 5, 52, 61, 66, 67, 69, 73, 83-97, 120
Celebrity Culture, 83-88, 93-97, 120

Celebrity Endorsements, 73, 74, 87, 93
Collective identity, 91, 127
Columbian Exposition, 32
Commodification, 16, 25, 26, 35, 36, 39, 42, 80, 101, 115, 117, 134
Commodity exchange value (vs use value), 7, 24, 34
Commodity fetishism, 7, 23-25, 33, 34, 36, 102, 107
Community, 57, 59, 60, 62, 82, 115, 134
Consumer Behavior, 29
Consumer Choice, 50, 62
Consumer culture, 1, 3-11, 13-21, 23-35, 37-39, 41-47, 49-52, 56-75, 77-97, 99-110, 112, 114-116, 118-125, 127-134
Consumer Ethics, 25, 91, 116, 119, 123
Consumer Goods and identity, 51, 57, 59, 102, 121
Consumer Products, 11, 51, 59
Consumer Psychology, 87
Consumer Rights, 110-113, 124, 129, 134
Consumer Trends, 20, 81, 99, 103, 109, 128
Corporate Capitalism, 116, 118
Counterculture, 103, 131
Cracker Barrel, 10-12, 15, 16
Credit, 67, 118
Critical Theory, 13, 39-41, 45, 58
Cultural Diversity, 18, 51, 72, 79, 104,

129, 132, 134
Cultural Evolution, 29
Cultural Homogenization, 13, 44
Cultural Identity, 53, 59, 71, 108
Cultural Intermediaries, 52, 55, 101
Cultural Memory, 88
Cultural Narratives, 45
Cultural Products, 1, 43
Cultural Resistance, 125, 131
Culture industry, the, 7, 39-41, 55, 57-
59, 67, 70, 71, 84, 108, 119, 121, 122, 130,
131
Cyberculture, 77, 79

D

Darwin, Charles, 115-117
De Tocqueville, Alexis, 113, 114, 117
DeBord, Guy, 63, 88
Debt, 67, 118, 122, 124
Democracy, 59, 110, 113, 114, 117, 124, 127,
134
Department stores, 3, 4, 9, 26, 27, 30, 31,
37, 38
Depthlessness, 57, 59
Disney, 3, 4, 10, 73, 74
Disneyfication, 8

E

Economic Growth, 1, 9, 10, 16, 29, 44,
62, 81, 86, 91, 105-107, 110, 114, 118, 120,
128, 131-133
Economic Ideologies, 109
Economic Models, 11, 12, 14, 17, 19, 46,
52, 53, 60, 61, 63-65, 89, 93, 96
Economic Power, 111
Economic Systems, 26, 106
Emerson, Ralph Waldo, 115, 116
Enlightenment, The, 28, 29, 39, 43, 44,
103, 110, 112, 118
Environmental Concerns, 133
Expositions, 3, 31, 32

F

Fashion, 17, 20, 29, 30, 33-35, 50-52, 56-
59, 63, 65, 72, 73, 89, 90, 97, 101, 102,
104, 105, 131
Flâneur, 35, 37, 38, 103
Ford, Henry, 118, 121
Frankfurt School, The, 25, 38, 41, 102
Freedom, 12, 55, 61, 69, 79, 80, 82, 86,
90-92, 108, 109, 113, 124, 127, 129, 131,
132, 134

G

Galbraith, John Kenneth, 41, 122
Global Capitalism, 79
Globalization, 13, 17, 18
Gloss, The, 9

H

Harrington, James, 111, 112
Horkheimer, Max, 38, 39, 67, 70
Hyper-Reality, 64, 77, 78, 96, 97, 99,
100, 102, 106

I

Identity and Culture, 59, 71, 108
Identity Creation, 51, 53
Identity Politics, 108
Ideological Constructs, 7, 14, 40, 54, 55,
58, 59, 61, 63, 75, 84-86, 107-125, 127,
128, 130, 133, 134
Illusion of choice, 10, 50, 60-62, 122, 123,
125, 132-134
Individual Choices, 60, 123, 132
Individualism, 21, 85, 86, 102, 104-106,
110, 112-117, 124, 127-130, 132, 134
Individuality, 14, 15, 50, 83, 102
Information Age, 42, 79, 80
Instrumental reason, 44, 117

J

Jameson, Fredric, 43, 106

K

Kellner, Douglas, 13, 14, 17, 45, 63
King of Prussia Mall, 3, 4
Kitsch, 72, 90

L

Laissez-faire, 110, 112, 114, 115, 124
Late capitalism, 43, 106
Leisure, role in identity, 121
Lifestyle Choices, 14, 15, 17, 18, 20, 21, 51, 52, 57, 60, 101, 103, 104, 121
Locke, John, 10, 61, 111, 112
Lucas, George, 73, 74
Lukács, Georg, 25
Lyotard, Jean-François, 44, 45

M

Marcuse, Herbert, 25
Market Dynamics, 50
Marx, Karl, 1, 2, 6-8, 21, 23-25, 28, 34-36, 39, 41, 49, 58, 75, 102, 107, 108, 119, 121, 130
Mass Consumption, 12, 16, 26, 103
Mass Media, 26, 39, 41, 70, 120
Mass Production, 16, 26, 30, 31, 46, 121
Material Culture, 10, 86, 109
Materialism, 6, 8, 104, 122, 125, 127, 131
McDonald's, 10, 13-18, 45
McDonaldization, 13, 14, 17, 18
Media Criticism, 88
Media Culture, 14, 39, 63, 70, 79, 88, 120
Media Representation, 93
Media Saturation, 13
Modernism, 14, 15, 17, 28, 31, 34, 38, 39, 42-45, 47, 49, 50, 56, 57, 59, 64, 70, 85, 96, 105, 132

N

Nostalgia, use of , 11, 12, 16, 55, 71, 90, 105

P

Pastiche, 64, 105
Paxton, Joseph, 31
Personal Freedom, 124
Personal Identity, 21, 51, 57, 59, 60, 67, 72, 102, 104, 110, 123, 131
Phantasmagoria, 31, 33-38
Political Economy, 21, 24
Political Ideologies, 75, 109
Popular Culture, 1, 3, 5, 7, 8, 10, 13, 16-19, 23, 27, 30, 32, 39, 41, 43, 47, 56-58, 63, 68, 72, 75, 78, 83, 84, 91, 94, 95, 97, 100-102, 105, 115, 129
Postmodernism, 15, 26-28, 31, 42-44, 50, 51, 56, 64, 65, 70, 96, 97, 101-106, 120, 123, 129
Product Marketing, 74, 93
Progress, 3, 5, 6, 15, 20, 21, 24, 29, 31, 33, 41, 44, 86, 96, 107, 110-112, 116, 119, 120, 123, 124, 133
Protestantism/Puritan work ethic, 28, 29, 59, 111, 121-123
Psychological Manipulation, 5, 7, 11, 12, 14, 39, 41, 55, 68, 81, 94, 96, 108
Public Good, 84, 113, 122
Public Space, 81, 96

R

Race and Consumerism, 14, 55, 111, 116
Rationality, 14, 38, 49, 94
Romanticism, 28
Rorty, Richard, 103

S

Self-Expression, 14, 50, 51, 58, 129
Shopping Malls, 3-5, 8, 9, 21, 30, 37, 38, 78, 94, 99, 102
Simulacra, 46, 47, 96

Smith, Adam, 111, 112
Social Criticism, 45, 52
Social Darwinism, 115
Social Fabric vs. Isolation, 35, 36, 113, 127
Social Identity, 108, 110
Social Ideology, 107, 110
Social Justice, 61, 95, 114
Social Mobility, 28, 29, 50, 110, 116
Social Movements, 81
Social Responsibility, 117, 128
Social Status, 123
Spectacle, 3, 4, 12, 18, 19, 21, 25, 26, 30, 35, 38, 49, 56, 63, 64, 66, 72, 74, 85, 87-89, 91, 93, 96, 125, 128-130, 134
Spencer, Herbert, 115, 116
Status Symbols, 1, 18-20, 39, 40, 50-53, 55, 58-60, 65, 66, 72, 73, 83-85, 88, 90-92, 94-96, 101, 102, 104, 107, 109, 123, 124, 130, 131
Styles, 5, 11, 15, 30, 49-52, 55, 56, 58, 65, 68, 72, 80, 90, 91, 97, 102-105, 123, 130
Suburbanization, 3, 4, 49
Surplus Value, 24
Symbolism, 58, 69, 95, 132

T

Technological Advancement, 68, 78

Television, 3-5, 16, 19, 41, 51, 63-75, 79, 86, 87, 90-93, 100, 101, 105, 130
Theories of Consumer Culture, 7

U

Urbanization, 85, 117, 121

V

Values, 12, 14, 20, 21, 23, 38, 40, 52, 59, 83, 84, 91, 103, 106, 107, 109, 110, 118, 119, 122, 125, 129
Veblen, Thorstein, 28
Virtual Reality, 77, 79

W

Wealth Distribution, 80
Weber, Max, 28, 117
Wilde, Oscar, 103
World's Fairs, 31

Y

Youth Culture, 56, 91

Printed in the United States
by Baker & Taylor Publisher Services